Author's Note

When the proposal for *Crossing the Chasm* was under negotiation, both the publisher and the author agreed that if the book sold more than five thousand copies, it would be doing well. After all, it was a niche book from an unknown author addressed to the somewhat esoteric challenges of marketing high-tech products.

In fact, by the end of the decade, the book had sold more than three hundred thousand copies since its first publication in 1991. Of course, publisher and author were delighted. But the more interesting question might be, Why was the book so successful? The answer is a textbook example of the effectiveness of word-of-mouth marketing, the very practice that the book advocates in its niche approach to gaining mainstream adoption for disruptive innovations.

First of all, it turned out that the metaphor of the chasm and the recommendations for how to cross it struck a deep chord among experienced high-tech managers. Countless readers have told me that, although they valued the material in the book, it really didn't tell them anything they didn't know already. Rather it captured what had been for them scattered intuitions and rueful learnings and put them into a coherent set of frameworks that could be used for future decision making.

This, in turn, caused them to pass the book along to colleagues, as much to spread the vocabulary as anything else. Thus the book left the marketing department and began to find its way to the engineering section, where a whole lot of readers claimed it was the first marketing book they didn't throw away after reading the early chapters. Praise from engineers is praise indeed, and the author was deeply grateful for this response.

This unusual turn of events also caught the eye of the venture capital community, which became a channel for more book sales. Venture capitalists saw in the new vocabulary a means to begin a market development dialogue with their engineering-oriented entrepreneurs. Indeed for whole companies the book became required reading, just to get everyone on the same page.

Professors at business schools then picked it up for their courses in entrepreneurial marketing, which was becoming all the rage in the decade following the book's first release. Students liked the book because it was both descriptive and prescriptive in clear terms, largely because it communicates the core of its arguments through metaphors, mixed though they often may be. If you bought into the analogies, you pretty much had the essence of the book, and reading it was just a confirmation of what you already knew.

And so things went swimmingly until around 1997 or so, when students began asking, "Who is Ashton Tate or Cullinet? What is WordStar or Ingres?" The examples, which are key to any argument by analogy, had grown long in the tooth. And so a revised edition was published, keeping the arguments largely intact but substituting 1990s companies for their 1980s predecessors, further affirming the author's belief that chasms are a perennial feature of the tech sector's landscape.

And that has been pretty much the status quo for the last decade. Sales have continued apace. Counting foreign language editions, at the time of this revision, they have surpassed six hundred thousand copies, with the frameworks in the book continuing to be invoked in the same contexts as before. But again, somewhere around 2007 students began asking, "Who was ChannelPoint? Who is VerticalNet? Silicon Graphics? Savi? Aren't there any case studies of companies we *actually know*?" And so, once again, it has become time to refresh the examples, a task that I embrace with enthusiasm, if perhaps a bit belatedly.

As before, my approach has been to preserve the fabric of the original book. To be sure, much water has passed under the bridge in the past decade, but once you start remodeling the bridge, you end up having to reconstruct it end to end. Instead, what I have allowed myself to do is add two appendices. The first is a short recap of the argument of the book which followed *Crossing the Chasm*, namely *Inside the Tornado*, the goal of which was to flesh out in full the Technology Adoption Life Cycle end to end from the early market, the chasm, and the bowling alley, on to the tornado, Main Street, and post-adoption category maturity. This should allow first-time readers to put crossing the chasm itself into its broader context.

The second appendix addresses arguably the most dramatic development in high tech of this century, the rise of consumer IT driven largely by increasingly innovative uses of mobile devices, cloud computing, and the World Wide Web. Prior to this era, IT categories almost always began life as business-to-business affairs with a subset eventually trickling down to business-to-consumer markets after the technology had been proven and cost reduced. But in this century, it has been the B2C businesses that have led the way, and it is just now that the B2B players are reaching out to bring these technologies into the enterprise.

It turns out that *Crossing the Chasm* is at heart a B2B market development model. It can be applied to B2C, at times quite effectively, but at the end of the day, it is not normally the best model to use. Instead, a model we have been calling the Four Gears has proved more useful for digital entrepreneurs building consumer businesses. So that is the topic addressed in the second appendix.

All in all, it has been quite a journey. Throughout, I have enjoyed the support of my family, especially my wife, Marie, as well as that of my many colleagues at the Chasm Group, Chasm Institute, TCG Advisors, and Mohr Davidow Ventures. Add to these my editors from HarperBusiness, my agent, Jim Levine, and my personal assistant and business manager, Pat Granger, and you can see it really does take a village. That said, perhaps most impactful of all have been the hundreds of clients who have brought to our consulting engagements the most interesting problems and the most engaging energy. They are the ones who inspire us all.

Geoffrey Moore
June 2013

CROSSING THE CHASM

CROSSING THE CHASM

Marketing and Selling Disruptive Products to Mainstream Customers

THIRD EDITION

Geoffrey A. Moore

HARPER
BUSINESS

An Imprint of HarperCollins*Publishers*
www.harpercollins.com

CROSSING THE CHASM, THIRD EDITION. Copyright © 1991, 1999, 2002, 2014 by Geoffrey A. Moore. All rights reserved. Printed in the United States of America. No part of this book may be used or reproduced in any manner whatsoever without written permission except in the case of brief quotations embodied in critical articles and reviews. For information, address HarperCollins Publishers, 195 Broadway , New York, NY 10007. HarperCollins books may be purchased for educational, business, or sales promotional use. For information, please e-mail the Special Markets Department at SPsales@harpercollins.com.

Originally published in hardcover in 1991 by HarperBusiness, an imprint of HarperCollins Publishers.

Clip art on page 243 courtesy of Cliparto Ltd. ("Vector-Images.com")

THIRD EDITION—2014

Library of Congress Cataloging-in-Publication Data has been applied for.

ISBN: 978-0-06-229298-8

20   OV/LSC   20 19 18 17 16 15

To Marie

Contents

PART ONE

Discovering the Chasm

Introduction

If Mark Zuckerberg Can Be a Billionaire

There is a line from a song in the musical *A Chorus Line*: "If Troy Donahue can be a movie star, then I can be a movie star." Every year one imagines hearing a version of this line reprised in high-tech start-ups across the country: "If Mark Zuckerberg can be a billionaire . . ." For indeed, the great thing about high tech is that, despite numerous disappointments, it still holds out the siren lure of a legitimate get-rich-quick opportunity.

This is the great attraction. And yet, as the Bible warns, while many are called, few are chosen. Every year millions of dollars— not to mention countless work hours of our nation's best technical talent—are lost in failed attempts to join this kingdom of the elect. And oh what wailing then, what gnashing of teeth!

"Why me?" cries out the unsuccessful entrepreneur. Or rather, "Why *not* me?" "Why not us?" chorus his equally unsuccessful investors. "Look at our product. Is it not as good— nay, better—than the product that beat us out? How can you say that Salesforce is better than RightNow, LinkedIn is better than Plaxo, Akamai's content delivery network is better than Internap's, or that Rackspace's cloud is better than Terremark's?"

How, indeed? For in fact, <u>feature for feature, the less successful</u> <u>product is often arguably superior.</u>

Not content to slink off the stage without some revenge, this sullen and resentful crew casts about among themselves to find a scapegoat, and whom do they light upon? With unfailing consistency and unerring accuracy, all fingers point to—*the vice president of marketing.* It <u>is marketing's fault!</u> Salesforce outmarketed RightNow, LinkedIn outmarketed Plaxo, Akamai outmarketed Internap, Rackspace outmarketed Terremark. Now we too have been outmarketed. Firing is too good for this monster. Hang him!

While this sort of thing takes its toll on the marketing profession, there is more at stake in these failures than a bumpy executive career path. When a high-tech venture fails, everyone goes down with the ship—not only the investors but also the engineers, the manufacturers, the president, and the receptionist. All those extra hours worked in hopes of cashing in on an equity option—all gone.

Worse still, because there is no obvious reason why one venture succeeds and the next one fails, the sources of capital to fund new products and companies become increasingly wary of investing. Interest rates go up, valuations go down, and the willingness to entertain venture risk abates. Meanwhile, Wall Street just emits another deep sigh. It has long been at wit's end when it comes to high-tech stocks. Despite the efforts of some of its best analysts, these stocks are traditionally misvalued, often spectacularly so, and therefore exceedingly volatile. It is not uncommon for a high-tech company to announce even a modest shortfall in its quarterly projections and incur a 30 percent devaluation in stock price on the following day of trading. As the kids like to say, What's up with that?

There are, however, even more serious ramifications. High-tech innovation and marketing expertise are two cornerstones of the U.S. strategy for global competitiveness. We will never have the lowest cost of labor or raw materials, so we must continue to exploit advantages further up the value chain. If we cannot at least learn to predictably and successfully bring high-tech products to market, our countermeasures against the onslaught of commoditizing globalization will falter, placing our entire standard of living in jeopardy.

With so much at stake, the erratic results of high-tech marketing are particularly frustrating, especially in a society where other forms of marketing appear to be so well under control. Elsewhere—in cars or consumer electronics or apparel—we may see ourselves being outmanufactured, but not outmarketed. Indeed, even after we have lost an entire category of goods to offshore competition, we remain the experts in marketing these goods to U.S. consumers. Why haven't we been able to apply these same skills to high tech? And what is it going to take for us to finally get it right?

It is the purpose of this book to answer these two questions in considerable detail. But the short answer is as follows: Our default model for how to develop a high-tech market is almost—but not quite—right. As a result, our marketing ventures, despite normally promising starts, drift off course in puzzling ways, eventually causing unexpected and unnerving gaps in sales revenues, and sooner or later leading management to undertake some desperate remedy. Occasionally these remedies work out, and the result is a high-tech marketing success. (Of course, when these are written up in retrospect, what was learned in hindsight is not infrequently portrayed as foresight, with the result that no one sees how perilously close to the edge the enterprise veered.) More often, however, the remedies either flat-out fail, and a product or a company goes belly-up, or they progress after a fashion to some kind of limp but yet-still-breathing half-life, in which the company has long since abandoned its dreams of success and contents itself with once again making payroll.

None of this is necessary. We have enough high-tech marketing history now to see where our model has gone wrong and how to fix it. To be specific, the point of greatest peril in the development of a high-tech market lies in making the transition from an *early market* dominated by a few *visionary* customers to a *mainstream market* dominated by a large block of customers who are predominantly *pragmatists* in orientation. The gap between these two markets, all too frequently ignored, is in fact so significant as to warrant being called a *chasm*, and crossing this chasm must be the primary focus of any long-term high-tech marketing plan. A successful crossing is how high-tech fortunes are made; failure in the attempt is how they are lost.

For the past two decades, I, along with my colleagues at the Chasm Group, Chasm Institute, and TCG Advisors, have watched countless companies struggle to maintain their footing during this difficult period. It is an extremely difficult transition for reasons that will be summarized in the opening chapters of this book. The good news is that there are reliable guiding principles. The material that follows has been refined over hundreds of consulting engagements focused on bringing products and companies into profitable and sustainable mainstream markets. The models presented here have been tested again and again and have been found effective. The chasm, in short, can be crossed.

That said, like a hermit crab that has outgrown its shell, the company crossing the chasm must scurry to find its new home.

Until it does, it will be vulnerable to all kinds of predators. This urgency means that everyone in the company—not just the marketing and sales people—must focus all their efforts on this one end until it is accomplished. Chapters 3 through 7 set forth the principles necessary to guide high-tech ventures during this period of great risk. This material focuses primarily on marketing, because that is where the leadership must come from, but I ultimately argue in the Conclusion that leaving the chasm behind requires significant changes throughout the high-tech enterprise. The book closes, therefore, with a call for additional new strategies in the areas of finance, organizational development, and R&D.

This book is unabashedly about and written specifically for marketing within high-tech enterprises. But high tech can be viewed as a microcosm of larger industrial sectors. In this context, the relationship between an early market and a mainstream market is not unlike the relationship between a fad and a trend. Marketing has long known how to exploit fads and how to develop trends. The problem, since these techniques are antithetical to each other, is that you need to decide which one—fad or trend—you are dealing with before you start. It would be much better if you could start with a fad, exploit it for all it was worth, and then turn it into a trend.

That may seem like a miracle, but that is in essence what high-tech marketing is all about. Every truly innovative high-tech product starts out as a fad—something with no known market value or purpose but with "great properties" that generate a lot of enthusiasm within an "in crowd" of early adopters. That's the early market.

Then comes a period during which the rest of the world watches to see if anything can be made of this; that is the chasm.

If in fact something does come out of it—if a value proposition is discovered that can be predictably delivered to a targetable set of customers at a reasonable price—then a new mainstream market segment forms, typically with a rapidity that allows its initial leaders to become very, very successful.

The key in all this is crossing the chasm—performing the acts that allow the first shoots of that mainstream market to emerge. This is a do-or-die proposition for high-tech enterprises; hence it is logical that they be the crucible in which "chasm theory" is formed. But the principles can be generalized to other forms of marketing, so for the general reader who can bear with all the high-tech examples in this book, useful lessons may be learned.

One of the most important lessons about crossing the chasm is that the task ultimately requires achieving an unusual degree of company unity during the crossing period. This is a time when one should forgo the quest for eccentric marketing genius in favor of achieving an informed consensus among mere mortals. It is a time not for dashing and expensive gestures but rather for careful plans and cautiously rationed resources—a time not to gamble all on some brilliant coup but rather to focus everyone on pursuing a high-probability course of action and making as few mistakes as possible.

One of the functions of this book, therefore—and perhaps its most important one—is to open up the logic of marketing decision making during this period so that everyone on the management team can participate in the market development process. If prudence rather than brilliance is to be our guiding principle, then many heads are better than one. If market forces are going to be the guiding element in our strategy—and most organizations insist this is their goal—then their principles must be accessible to all the players, and not, as is sometimes the case, reserved to an elect few who have managed to penetrate their mysteries.

Crossing the Chasm, therefore, is written for the entire high-tech community—for everyone who is a stakeholder in the venture, engineers as well as marketers, and financiers as well. All must come to a common accord if the chasm is to be safely negotiated. And with that thought in mind, let us turn to chapter 1.

1

High-Tech Marketing Illusion

When this book was originally drafted in 1989, I drew on the example of an electric car as a disruptive innovation that had yet to cross the chasm. Indeed at that time there were only a few technology enthusiasts retrofitting cars with alternative power supplies. When I revised it extensively in 1999, once again I drew on the same example. GM had just released an electric vehicle, and all the other manufacturers were making noise. But the market yawned instead. Now it is 2013, and once again we are talking about the market for electric vehicles. This time the vendor in the spotlight is Tesla, and the vehicle getting the most attention is their Model S sedan.

Stepping back a bit from the cool factor, let's assume these cars work like any other, except they are quieter and better for the environment. Now the question is: When are you going to buy one?

The Technology Adoption Life Cycle

Your answer to the preceding question will tell a lot about how you relate to the *Technology Adoption Life Cycle*, a model for understanding the acceptance of new products. If your answer is "Not until hell freezes over," you are probably a very late adopter of technology, what we call in the model a *laggard*. If your answer is "When I have seen electric cars prove themselves and when there are enough service stations on the road," you might be a middle-of-the-road adopter, or in the model, the *early majority*. If you say, "Not until most people have made the switch and it becomes really inconvenient to drive a gasoline car," you are probably more of a follower, a member of the *late majority*. If, on the other hand, you want to be the first one on your block with an electric car, you are apt to be an *innovator* or an *early adopter*.

In a moment we are going to take a look at these labels in greater detail, but first we need to understand their significance. It turns out our attitude toward technology adoption becomes significant—at least in a marketing sense—any time we are introduced to products that require us to change our current mode of behavior or to modify other products and services we rely on. In academic terms, such change-sensitive products are called *discontinuous* or *disruptive innovations*. The contrasting term, *continuous* or *sustaining innovations*, refers to the normal upgrading of products that does not require us to change behavior.

For example, when Warby Parker promises you better-looking eyeglasses, that is a continuous innovation. You still are wearing the same combination of lenses and frames, you just look cooler. When Ford's Fusion promises better mileage, when Google Gmail promises you better integration with other Google apps, or when Samsung promises sharper and brighter TV pictures across bigger and bigger screens, these are all continuous innovations. As a consumer, you don't have to change your ways in order to take advantage of these improvements.

On the other hand, if the Samsung were a 3-D TV, it would be incompatible with normal viewing, requiring you to don special glasses to get the special effects. This would be a discontinuous innovation because you would have to change your normal TV-viewing behavior. Similarly if the new Gmail account were to be activated on a Google Chrome notebook running Android, it would be incompatible with most of today's software base, which runs under either Microsoft or Apple operating systems. Again, you would be required to seek out a whole new set of software, thereby classifying this too as a discontinuous innovation. Or if the new Ford Fusion is the Energi model, which uses electricity instead of gasoline, or if the new sight-improvement offer were Lasik surgery rather than eyeglasses, then once again you would have an offer incompatible with the infrastructure of supporting components otherwise available. In all these cases, the innovation demands significant changes by not only the consumer but also the infrastructure of supporting businesses that provide complementary products and services to round out the complete offer. That is how and why such innovations come to be called discontinuous.

Between *continuous* and *discontinuous* lies a spectrum of demands for behavioral change. Contact lenses, unlike Lasik surgery, do not require a whole new infrastructure, but they do ask for a whole new set of behaviors from the consumer. Internet TVs do not require any special viewing glasses, but they do require the consumer to be "digitally competent."

Microsoft's Surface tablet, unlike the Chrome notebook, is compatible with the installed base of Microsoft applications, but its "tiles" interface requires users to learn a whole new set of conventions. And Ford's hybrid Fusion, unlike its Energi model, can leverage the existing infrastructure of gas stations, but it does require learning new habits for starting and running the car. All these, like the special washing instructions for certain fabrics, the special street lanes reserved for bicycle riders, the special dialing instructions for calling overseas, represent some new level of demand on the consumer to absorb a change in behavior. That's the price of modernization. Sooner or later, all businesses must make these demands. And so it is that all businesses can profit by lessons from high-tech industries.

Whereas other industries introduce discontinuous innovations only occasionally and with much trepidation, high-tech enterprises do so routinely and as confidently as a born-again Christian holding four aces. From their inception, therefore, high-tech industries have needed a marketing model that coped effectively with this type of product introduction. Thus the Technology Adoption Life Cycle became central to the entire sector's approach to marketing. (People are usually amused to learn that the original research that gave rise to this model was done on the adoption of new strains of seed potatoes among American farmers. Despite these agrarian roots, however, the model has thoroughly transplanted itself into the soil of Silicon Valley.)

The model describes the market penetration of any new technology product in terms of a progression in the types of consumers it attracts throughout its useful life:

TECHNOLOGY ADOPTION LIFE CYCLE

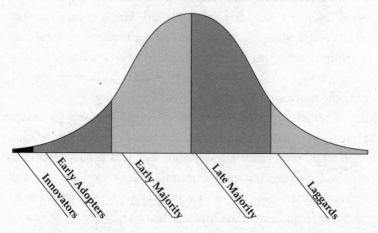

As you can see, we have a bell curve. The divisions in the curve are roughly equivalent to where standard deviations would fall. That is, the early majority and the late majority fall within one standard deviation of the mean, the early adopters and the laggards within two, and way out there, at the very onset of a new technology, about three standard deviations from the norm, are the innovators.

The groups are distinguished from each other by their characteristic response to a discontinuous innovation based on a new technology. Each group represents a unique *psychographic* profile—a combination of psychology and demographics that makes its marketing responses different from those of the other groups. Understanding each profile and its relationship to its neighbors provides a critical foundation for high-tech marketing overall.

Innovators pursue new technology products aggressively. They sometimes seek them out even before a formal marketing program has been launched. This is because technology is a central interest in their life, regardless of what function it is performing. At root they are intrigued with any fundamental advance and often make a technology purchase simply for the pleasure of exploring the new device's properties. There are not very many innovators in any given market segment, but winning them over at the outset of a marketing campaign is important nonetheless, because their endorsement reassures the other players in the marketplace that the product could in fact work.

Early adopters, like innovators, buy into new product concepts very early in their life cycle, but unlike innovators, they are not technologists. Rather they are people who find it easy to imagine, understand, and appreciate the benefits of a new technology, and to relate these potential benefits to their other concerns. Whenever they find a strong match, early adopters are willing to base their buying decisions upon it. Because early adopters do not rely on well-established references in making these buying decisions, preferring instead to rely on their own intuition and vision, they are core to opening up any high-tech market segment.

The early majority share some of the early adopter's ability to relate to technology, but ultimately they are driven by a strong sense of practicality. They know that many of these newfangled inventions end up as passing fads, so they are content to wait and see how other people are making out before they buy in themselves. They want to see well-established references before investing substantially. Because there are so many people in this segment— roughly one-third of the whole adoption life cycle—winning their business is fundamental to any substantial profits and growth.

The *late majority* shares all the concerns of the early majority, plus one major additional one: Whereas people in the early majority are comfortable with their ability to handle a technology product, should they finally decide to purchase it, members of the late majority are not. As a result, they wait until something has become an established standard, and even then they want to see lots of support and tend to buy, therefore, from large, well-established companies. Like the early majority, this group comprises about one-third of the total buying population in any given segment. Courting its favor is highly profitable indeed, for while profit margins decrease as the products mature, so do the selling costs, and virtually all the R&D costs have been amortized.

Finally there are the *laggards*. These people simply don't want anything to do with new technology, for any of a variety of reasons, some personal and some economic. The only time they ever buy a technological product is when it is buried deep inside another product—the way, say, that a microprocessor is designed into the braking system of a new car—such that they don't even know it is there. From a market development perspective laggards are generally regarded as not worth pursuing on any other basis.

To recap the logic of the Technology Adoption Life Cycle, its underlying thesis is that technology is absorbed into any given community in stages corresponding to the psychological and social profiles of various segments within that community. This process can be thought of as a continuum with definable stages, each associated with a definable group, and each group making up a predictable portion of the whole.

The High-Tech Marketing Model

This profile is in turn the very foundation of the High-Tech Marketing Model. That model says that the way to develop a high-tech market is to work the curve left to right, focusing first on the innovators, growing that market segment, then moving on to the early adopters, growing that segment, and so on, to the early majority, late majority, and even to the laggards. In this effort, companies must use each "captured" group as a reference base for launching their marketing into the next group. Thus the endorsement of innovators becomes an important tool for developing a credible pitch to the early adopters, that of the early adopters to the early majority, and so on.

The idea is to keep this process moving smoothly, progressing something like the passing of a baton in a relay race or like Tarzan making his way across the jungle swinging from vine to well-placed vine. It is important to maintain momentum in order to create a bandwagon effect that makes it natural for the next group to want to buy in. Too much of a delay and the effect would be something like hanging from a motionless vine—nowhere to go but down. (Actually, going down is the graceful alternative. What happens more often is a desperate attempt to re-create momentum, typically through some highly visible form of promotion, which ends up making the company look like Tarzan frantically jerking back and forth, trying to get a vine moving with no leverage. This typically leads the other animals in the jungle just to sit and wait for him to fall.)

There is an additional motive for maintaining momentum: to keep ahead of the next emerging technology. In the past decade desktop personal computers have largely been displaced by laptops, a substantial number of which are likely to be displaced in this decade by tablets. You need to take advantage of your day in the sun before the next day renders you obsolete. From this notion comes the idea of a *window of opportunity*. If momentum is lost, then we can be overtaken by a competitor, thereby losing the advantages exclusive to a technology leadership position—specifically, the profit-margin advantage during the middle to late stages, which is the primary source from which high-tech fortunes are made.

This, in essence, is the High-Tech Marketing Model—a vision of a smooth unfolding through all the stages of the Technology Adoption Life Cycle. What is dazzling about this concept, particularly to those who own equity in a high-tech venture, is its promise of a virtual monopoly over a major new market development. If you can get there first, "catch the curve," and ride it up through the early majority segment, thereby establishing the de facto standard, you can get rich very quickly and "own" a highly profitable market for a very long time to come.

Testimonials

The Apple iPad is a prime example of leveraging the High-Tech Marketing Model end to end. Launched in 2009 after being demoed at MacWorld by Steve Jobs, its touch-interface dynamics and gorgeous display of images made it an instant hit with Mac enthusiasts, selling three hundred thousand units its first day. Then visionary executives began using it as their personal digital assistant, especially for email and presentations, forcing their CIOs to find a way to accommodate them. Then sales executives, the ultimate pragmatists, found that iPads were great for one-on-one presentations to economic buyers, and now whole sales forces were getting outfitted. Meanwhile, in boardrooms across America the iPad had become a socially acceptable way to be always online, in part because one could distribute board materials to it electronically to be accessed during the meeting. Then the kids got their hands on them, and there was a massive explosion in use cases, primarily Facebook and other forms of social computing, but also including leveraging the World Wide Web for broader educational impact. And with Facebook along came the grandparents, historically a conservative if not a laggard constituency when it came to anything computer related. And finally it got to toddlers and babies, and God help us, kittens interacting directly with the screens and experiencing frustration with any image that fails to respond like an iPad. In sum, in less than five years, iPads have become pervasively integrated into the information fabric that makes up our digital lives—not bad for something not old enough to be in the first grade.

Astounding as this accomplishment is, many other companies have achieved a comparable status. This is what Microsoft, Intel, and Dell achieved in desktop PCs, Qualcomm and ARM in smartphones, Cisco in routers and switches, Google in search advertising, SAP in enterprise-class business applications, Oracle in relational databases, and HP in laser and inkjet printers.

Each of these companies has held market share in excess of 50 percent in its prime market. All of them have been able to establish strongholds in the early majority segment, if not beyond, and to this day look forward to continued growth, strong profit margins, and preferred relationships with suppliers and customers. To be sure, some like Dell and, more dramatically, HP have fallen on hard times, but even then customers often bend over backward to give market share leaders second and third chances, bringing cries of anguish from their competitors who would never be granted such grace.

It should come as no surprise that the history of these flagship products conforms to the High-Tech Marketing Model. In truth, the model was essentially derived from an abstraction of these histories. And so high-tech marketing, well into the second decade of the twenty-first century, keeps before it the example of these companies and the abstraction of the High-Tech Marketing Model, and marches confidently forward.

Of course, if that were a sufficient formula for success, you would need to read no further.

Illusion and Disillusion: Cracks in the Bell Curve

It is now time to advise you that there are any number of us in Silicon Valley who are willing to testify that there is something wrong with the High-Tech Marketing Model. We believe this to be true because we all own what once were meaningful equity stakes in corporations that either no longer exist or whose current valuation is so diluted that our stock—were there a market for it, which there is not—has lost all monetary significance.

Although we all experienced our fates uniquely, much of our shared experience can be summarized by recasting the Technology Adoption Life Cycle in the following way:

THE *REVISED* TECHNOLOGY ADOPTION LIFE CYCLE

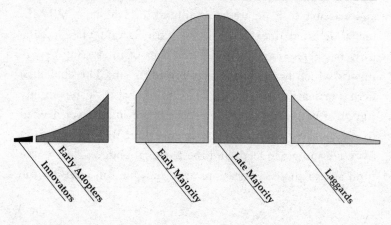

As you can see, the components of the life cycle are un-changed, but between any two psychographic groups has been introduced a gap. This symbolizes the dissociation between the two groups—that is, the difficulty any group will have in accepting a new product if it is presented in the same way as it was to the group to its immediate left. Each of these gaps rep-resents an opportunity for marketing to lose momentum, to miss the transition to the next segment, thereby never to gain the promised land of profit-margin leadership in the middle of the bell curve.

The First Crack

Two of the gaps in the High-Tech Marketing Model are rela-tively minor—what one might call "cracks in the bell curve"—yet even here unwary ventures have slipped and fallen. The first is between the innovators and the early adopters. It is a gap that occurs when a hot technology product cannot be readily trans-lated into a major new benefit—something like Esperanto. The enthusiast loves it for its architecture, but nobody else can even figure out how to start using it.

Take virtual reality, for example. It is very cool technology and was able to generate its own mark-up language, VRML, but aside from one early success with Second Life, it basi-cally has been characterized by a series of interesting exper-iments which have yet to be followed up on. The challenge here is primarily technological, meaning that the gap is simply too great between the Google-class processing power needed to create a truly seamless experience (our neurons are very fussy consumers indeed) and the personal budgets that would fund any of these applications at scale. One can envision the technology getting there someday, but for now that day is so far in the future, it leaves virtual reality stuck with the enthusiasts waiting for a visionary.

The same could be said for 3-D printing. This has inspired a generation of technology enthusiasts to form a "Maker's Movement," an extension of the do-it-yourself culture that specializes in fabricating objects of all sorts. At the time of this writing 3-D printing is getting a lot of press, but the actual market is still much like the original home computing market in the days of Heathkits before the Apple II—a DIY technology enthusiast's paradise.

This is a market development problem. As we shall see in the next chapter, the key to getting beyond the enthusiasts and winning over a visionary is to show that the new technology enables some strategic leap forward, something never before possible, which has an intrinsic value and appeal to the nontechnologist. This benefit is typically symbolized by a single, compelling *flagship application*, something that showcases the power and value of the new product. If the marketing effort is unable to find that compelling application, then market development stalls with the innovators, and the future of the product falls through this first crack in the bell curve.

The Other Crack

There is another crack in the bell curve, of approximately equal magnitude, that falls between the early majority and the late majority. By this point in the Technology Adoption Life Cycle, the market is already well developed, and the technology product has been absorbed into the mainstream. The key issue now—transitioning from the early to the late majority—has to

do with lingering residual demands on the end user to be technologically competent.

Simply put, the early majority is willing and able to become
technologically competent where necessary; the late majority is
not. When a product reaches this point in the market development, it must be made increasingly easier to adopt in order to
continue being successful. If this does not occur, the transition
to the late majority will stall.

Home automation, programmable appliances, and high-end
cameras are all currently in this situation, as are a whole slew of
telephones that offer call forwarding, three-way conferencing,
or even just call transferring. How many times have you been
on the phone and heard—or said—"Now I may lose you when I
hit the transfer button, so be sure to call back if I do." The problem is that for people who are not frequent users of the system
the protocols are simply too hard to remember. As a result, users
do not use the features, and so companies in mature markets
find it harder and harder to get paid for the R&D they have
done because the end user cannot capture the benefit. Instead,
they bemoan that the product has become a commodity when
in fact it is the *experience* of the product that has been com-
moditized. This truly is marketing's fault, particularly when
companies have ceded marketing the right to redesign the user
interface and thus control the user experience.

Other examples of products in danger of falling through
the crack between the early and late majority are scanning and
project management software. The market leaders in these two
areas, Hewlett-Packard and Microsoft respectively, have been
quite successful in capturing the early majority, but their products still give conservatives in the late majority pause. And so

these categories are in danger of stagnating although neither market has ever in fact been saturated.

Discovering the Chasm

The real news, however, is not the two cracks in the bell curve, the one between the innovators and the early adopters, the other between the early and late majority. No, the real news is the deep and dividing *chasm* that separates the early adopters from the early majority. This is by far the most formidable and unforgiving transition in the Technology Adoption Life Cycle, and it is all the more dangerous because it typically goes unrecognized.

The reason the transition can go unnoticed is that with both groups the customer list and the size of the order can look the same. Typically, in either segment, you would see a list of Fortune 500 to Fortune 2000 customers making relatively large orders—five figures for sure, more often six figures or even higher. But in fact the basis for the sale—what has been promised, implicitly or explicitly, and what must be delivered—is radically different.

What the early adopter is buying, as we shall see in greater detail in Chapter 2, is some kind of *change agent*. By being the first to implement this change in their industry, the early adopters expect to get a jump on the competition, whether from lower product costs, faster time to market, more complete customer service, or some other comparable business advantage. They expect a radical discontinuity between the old ways and the new, and they are prepared to champion this cause against entrenched resistance. Being the first, they also are prepared to bear with the inevitable bugs and glitches that accompany any innovation just coming to market.

By contrast, the early majority want to buy a *productivity improvement* for existing operations. They are looking to minimize the discontinuity with the old ways. They want evolution, not revolution. They want technology to enhance, not overthrow, the established ways of doing business. And above all, they do not want to debug somebody else's product. By the time they adopt it, they want it to work properly and to integrate appropriately with their existing technology base.

This contrast just scratches the surface relative to the differences and incompatibilities among early adopters and the early majority. Let me just make two key points for now: Because of these incompatibilities, early adopters do not make good references for the early majority. And because of the early majority's concern not to disrupt their organizations, good references are critical to their buying decisions. So what we have here is a catch-22. The only suitable reference for an early majority customer, it turns out, is another member of the early majority, but no upstanding member of the early majority will buy without first having consulted with several suitable references.

Bodies in the Chasm

What happens in this catch-22 situation? First, because the product *has* caught on with the early adopters, it has garnered a lot of publicity: Holograms, pen-based tablets, fuel cells, QR codes, Massive Open Online Courses—we have all read a lot about these types of offerings, yet not one has achieved to date mainstream market status, despite the fact that the current offers actually do work reasonably well. In large part this is because of the high degree of discontinuity implicit in their adoption by organizations, and the inability of the marketing effort, to date, to lower this barrier to the early majority. So the products languish, continuing to feed off the early adopter segment of the market, but unable to really take off and break through to the high-volume opportunities.

Segways are a classic example of this phenomenon. You've seen them on occasion in malls or in airports, looking something like an old-fashioned lawn mower gone vertical, ridden around by someone in a security professional's uniform. Kind of dorky looking, but don't kid yourself. The gyroscopic balance control is fabulous, and the control movements once mastered are graceful. The hope was these devices would become a universal transport mechanism. Why didn't that happen? In a word: *stairs*. Stairs are pesky little devils that crop up everywhere, and Segways do not handle them well at all. That's what we call a showstopper. So while Steve Wozniak can still field a brace of Segways for a rousing match of polo, no one has yet come up with a breakthrough application for the rest of us. Hence its fate for any foreseeable future is to dwell in the chasm forever.

As expensive a lesson as the Segway was for its investors, it pales by comparison with the reputed $6 billion bath Motorola took on its satellite mobile phone venture Iridium. Again, from a technology enthusiast's point of view, what a great idea! Instead of building out tens of thousands of cellular base stations everywhere—and still failing to adequately cover sparsely populated areas—how about putting up seventy-seven low-earth-orbiting satellites and do the job for the entire planet? (FYI, seventy-seven happens to be the atomic number for iridium, which is a technology enthusiast's idea of a cool inside joke.) So what happened? Well, in this case it was not stairs that were the problem, it was *buildings*! Satellite communications do not work very well inside buildings. Add to that the bulkiness of the handsets compared to cellular mobile phones, plus the very high cost of subscribing, and once again you have a showstopper. Today the technology is indeed used successfully for niche applications, but to put that in perspective, the network was bought out of bankruptcy for $25 million. Chasms can result in very painful falls indeed.

In sum, when promoters of high-tech products try to make the transition from a market base made up of visionary early adopters to penetrate the next adoption segment, the pragmatist early majority, they are effectively operating *without a reference base and without a support base within a market that is highly reference oriented and highly support oriented.*

This is indeed a chasm, and into this chasm many an unwary start-up venture has fallen. Despite repeated instances of the chasm effect, however, high-tech marketing still struggles to get this problem properly in focus. As a final prelude to our going forward, therefore, by way of evoking additional glimmers of recognition and understanding of this plight of the chasm, I offer the following parable as a kind of condensation of the entrepreneurial experience gone awry.

A High-Tech Parable

In the first year of selling a product—most of it alpha and beta release—the emerging high-tech company expands its customer list to include some technology enthusiast innovators and one or two visionary early adopters. Everyone is pleased, and at the first annual Christmas party, held on the company premises, plastic glasses and potluck canapés are held high.

In the second year—the first year of true product—the company wins over several more visionary early adopters, including a handful of truly major deals. Revenue meets plan, and everyone is convinced it is time to ramp up—especially the venture capitalists who note that next year's plan calls for a 300 percent increase in revenue. (What could justify such a number? The High Tech Marketing Model, of course! For are we not just at that point in the model where the slope will increase exponentially? We don't want to lose market share at this critical juncture to some competitor. We must exploit our first-mover advantage and act while we are still within our window of opportunity. Strike while the iron is hot!) This year the company Christmas party is held at a fine hotel, the glasses are crystal, the wine vintage, and the theme, à la Dickens, is "Great Expectations."

At the beginning of the third year, a major sales force expansion is undertaken, impressive sales collateral and advertising are underwritten, district offices are opened, and customer support is strengthened. Halfway through the year, however, sales revenues are disappointing. A few more companies have come on board, but only after a prolonged sales struggle and significant compromise on price. The number of sales overall is far fewer than expected, and growth in expenses is vastly outdistancing growth in income. In the meantime, R&D is badly bogged down with several special projects committed to in the early contracts with the original customers.

Meetings are held (for the young organization is nothing if not participative in its management style). The salespeople complain that there are great holes in the product line and that what is available today is overpriced, full of bugs, and not what the customer wants. The engineers claim they have met spec and schedule for every major release, at which point the customer support staff merely groan. Executive managers lament that the sales force doesn't call high enough in the prospect organization, lacks the ability to communicate the vision, and simply isn't aggressive enough. Nothing is resolved, and, off line, political enclaves begin to form.

Third quarter revenues results are in—and they are absolutely dismal. It is time to whip the slaves. The board of venture capitalists starts in on the founders and the president, who in turn put the screws to the vice president of sales, who passes it on to the troops in the trenches. Turnover follows. The vice president of marketing is fired. It's time to bring in "real management." More financing is required, with horrendous dilution for the initial cadre of investors—especially the founders and the key technical staff. One or more founders object but are shunted aside. Six months pass. Real management doesn't do any better. Key defections occur. Time to bring in consultants. More turnover. What we really need now, investors decide, is a turnaround artist. Layoffs followed by more turnover. And so it goes. When the screen fades to the credits, yet another venture staggers off to join the twilight companies of Silicon Valley—zombie enterprises, not truly alive and yet, due in part to the vagaries of venture capital accounting, unable to choose death with dignity.

Now, it is possible that this parable overstates the case—I have been accused of such things in the past. But it is no exaggeration to say that year in and year out, hundreds of high-tech start-ups, despite having good technology and exciting products, and despite initial promising returns from the market, falter and then fail. Here's why:

What the company staff interpreted as a ramp in sales leading smoothly "up the curve" was in fact an initial blip—what we will be calling the *early market*—and not the first indications of an emerging *mainstream market*. The company failed because its managers were unable to recognize that there is something fundamentally different between a sale to an early adopter and a sale to the early majority, even when the company name on the check reads the same. Thus, at a time of greatest peril, when the company was just entering the chasm, its leaders held high expectations rather than modest ones, and spent heavily in expansion projects rather than husbanding resources.

All this is the result of high-tech marketing illusion—the belief induced by the High-Tech Marketing Model that new markets unfold in a continuous and smooth way. In order to avoid the perils of the chasm, we need to achieve a new state—high-tech marketing enlightenment—by going deeper into the dynamics of the Technology Adoption Life Cycle to correct the flaws in the model and provide a secure basis for marketing strategy development.

2

High-Tech Marketing Enlightenment

First there is a mountain,
Then there is no mountain,
Then there is.

— Zen proverb

What is it about California? How can any state be so successful and yet so weird? I myself am from Oregon, a perfectly normal state, with a pleasantly thriving economy and plenty of fishermen and lumberjacks and such to balance out the high-tech crazies. I never intended to move south and write a book that says—in the very next paragraph, mind you—that you should bet your next million on a Zen proverb. California is a bad influence.

However, if you are going to risk time and money in high tech, then you really do need to remember how high-tech markets develop, and the following proverb is as good a way as any:

First there is a market . . . Made up of innovators and early adopters, it is an early market, flush with enthusiasm and vision and, often as not, funded by a potful of customer dollars earmarked for accomplishing some grand strategic goal.

Then there is no market . . . This is the chasm period, during which the early market is still trying to digest its ambitious projects, and the mainstream market waits to see if anything good will come of them.

Then there is. If all goes well, and the product and your company pass through the chasm period intact, then a mainstream market does emerge, made up of the early and the late majority. With them comes the real opportunity for wealth and growth.

To reap the rewards of the mainstream market, your marketing strategy must successfully respond to all three of these stages. In each case, the key to success is to focus in on the dominant "adoption type" in the current phase of the market, learn to appreciate that segment's psychographics, and then adjust your marketing strategy and tactics accordingly. Illustrating how to do that is the goal of this chapter.

First Principles

Before we get started, however, we need to establish some ground rules. The first step toward enlightenment is to get a firm grasp on the obvious. In our case, that means getting a useful working definition of the word *marketing*. Useful in this context means actionable—can we find in the concept of marketing a reasonable basis for taking actions that will predictably and positively affect company revenues? That, after all, is the purpose of this book.

Actually, in this context, defining marketing is not particularly difficult: It simply means taking actions to create, grow, maintain, or defend markets. What a market is we will get to in a moment, but it is, first, a real thing, independent of any one individual's actions. Marketing's purpose, therefore, is to develop and shape something that is real, and not, as people sometimes want to believe, to create illusions. In other words, we are dealing with a discipline more akin to gardening or sculpting than, say, to spray painting or hypnotism.

Of course, talking this way about marketing merely throws the burden of definition onto market, which we will define, for the purposes of high tech, as:

- a set of actual or potential customers
- for a given set of products or services
- who have a common set of needs or wants, and
- who reference each other when making a buying decision.

People intuitively understand every part of this definition except the last. Unfortunately, getting the last part—the notion that part of what defines a high-tech market is the tendency of its members to reference each other when making buying decisions—is absolutely key to successful high-tech marketing. So let's make this as clear as possible.

If two people buy the same product for the same reason but have no way they could reference each other, they are not part of the same market. That is, if I sell an oscilloscope for monitoring heartbeats to a doctor in Boston and the identical product for the same purpose to a doctor in Zaire, and these two doctors have no reasonable basis for communicating with each other, then I am dealing in two different markets. Similarly, if I sell an oscilloscope to a doctor in Boston and then go next door and sell the same product to an engineer working on a sonar device, I am also dealing in two different markets. In both cases, the reason we have separate markets is that the customers could not have referenced each other.

Depending on what day of the week it is, this idea seems to be either blindingly obvious or doubtful at best. Staying with the example at hand, can't one argue that there is, after all, such a thing as the oscilloscope market? Well, yes and no. If you want to use the word *market* in this sense (I would prefer you use the word *category* to convey this idea), it stands for the aggregate sales, both past and projected, for oscilloscopes. If that is how you want to use the word—say, if you are a financial analyst—that's fine, but you had better realize you are adding apples and oranges (that is, doctor sales + engineer sales) to get your final totals, and in so doing, you are leaving yourself open to misinterpreting the data badly. Most important, *market*, when it is defined in this sense, ceases to be a single, isolable object of action—it no longer refers to any single entity that can be acted on—and cannot, therefore, be the focus of marketing.

The way around this problem for many marketing professionals is to break up the category into isolable "market segments." *Market segments*, in this vocabulary, meet our definition of markets, including the self-referencing aspect. When marketing consultants sell market segmentation studies, all they are actually doing is breaking out the natural market boundaries within an aggregate of current and potential sales.

Marketing professionals insist on market segmentation because they know that no meaningful marketing program can be implemented across a set of customers who do not reference each other. The reason for this is simply leverage. No company can afford to pay for every marketing contact made. Every program must rely on some ongoing chain-reaction effects—what is usually called word of mouth. The more self-referencing the market and the more tightly bounded its communications channels, the greater the opportunity for such effects.

So much for first principles. There are additional elements to our final definition of market—principally, a concept called "the whole product"—but we will get to that later in the book. For now, let's apply what we have to the three phases of high-tech marketing. The first of these is the early market.

Early Markets

The initial customer set for a new technology product is made up primarily of innovators and early adopters. In the high-tech industry, the innovators are better known as technology enthusiasts or just techies, whereas the early adopters are the visionaries. It is the latter group, the visionaries, who dominate the buying decisions in this market, but it is the technology enthusiasts who are first to realize the potential in the new product. High-tech marketing, therefore, begins with the techies.

Innovators: The Technology Enthusiasts

Classically, the first people to adopt any new technology are those who appreciate the technology for its own sake. For anyone old enough to have been raised on Donald Duck comic books from Walt Disney (a dwindling cadre, to be sure), Gyro Gearloose may well have been your first encounter with a technology enthusiast. Or, if you were more classically educated, perhaps it was Archimedes crying, "Eureka!" at discovering the concept of measuring specific gravity through the displacement of water, or Daedalus, inventing a labyrinth and then the wings whereby one could fly out of it (if one did not fly too close to the sun). Or, for those who turn more toward movies and TV, more familiar examples of the type include *Back to the Future*'s Doc Brown or Data from *Star Trek*, or Sherlock Holmes as portrayed in the TV show *Elementary*. "Inventors," "propeller heads," "nerds," "techies"—we have many labels for a group of people who are, as a rule and despite a tendency toward introversion, delightful companions—provided you like to talk about technical topics.

They are the ones who first appreciate the architecture of your product and why it therefore has a competitive advantage over the current crop of products established in the marketplace. They are the ones who will spend hours trying to get products to work that, in all conscience, never should have been shipped in the first place. They will forgive ghastly documentation, horrendously slow performance, ludicrous omissions in functionality, and bizarrely obtuse methods of invoking some needed function—all in the name of moving technology forward. They make great critics because they truly care.

To give some high-tech examples, technology enthusiasts are the ones who buy HDTVs, home networking solutions, and digital cameras when they each cost well over a thousand dollars. They are interested in voice synthesis and voice recognition, interactive multimedia systems, neural networks, the modeling of chaos in Mandelbrot sets, and the notion of an artificial life based on silicon. At the moment I am writing this sentence they are logging on to Amazon Web Services with their credit card to test out their latest SETI hypothesis.

Sometimes a technology enthusiast becomes famous— usually as the inventor of a lucrative product. In the world of

PCs, Bill Gates started business life this way, but he may have forfeited his status somewhat as he became more Machiavellian. Marc Andreessen, on the other hand, has tried to stay more in role, although he too is looking more and more corporate. That could not be said, on the other hand, of such Internet founding stalwarts as Perl inventor Larry Wall, Apache cofounder Brian Behlendorf, or Linux creator Linus Torvalds. Birkenstocks forever, man. Power to the People (oops, sorry, I'm having a 1960's flashback).

My personal favorite, though, was a fellow named David Lichtman, with whom I worked at Rand Information Systems in the late seventies and early eighties. Long before anyone was taking PCs seriously, David showed me one he had put together himself—including, as a peripheral, a voice synthesizer. This was sitting on his desk at work right next to a little microprocessor-driven box he had invented to fill out his time sheet for him. If you followed David home, you would find a house littered with cameras, sound equipment, and assorted electronic toys. And at work, whenever there was any question about how a particularly arcane or intricate tool actually functioned, David was the man to ask. He was the archetypal technology enthusiast.

In business, technology enthusiasts are the gatekeepers for any new technology. They are the ones who have the interest to learn about it and the ones everyone else deems competent to do the early evaluation. As such, they are the first key to any high-tech marketing effort.

As a buying population, or as key influencers in corporate buying decisions, technology enthusiasts pose fewer requirements than any other group in the adoption profile—but you must not ignore the issues that are important to them. First, and most crucially, they want the truth, and without any tricks.

Second, wherever possible, whenever they have a technical problem, they want access to the most technically knowledgeable person to answer it. Often this may not be sound from a management point of view, and you will have to deny or restrict such access, but you should never forget that it is wanted.

Third, they want to be first to get the new stuff. By working with them under nondisclosure—a commitment to which they typically adhere scrupulously—you can get great feedback early in the design cycle and begin building a supporter who will influence buyers not only in his own company but elsewhere in the marketplace as well. Finally, they want everything cheap. This is sometimes a matter of budgets, but it is more fundamentally a problem of perception—they think all technology should be free or available at cost, and they have no use for "added-value" arguments. The key consequence here is, if it is their money, you have to make it available cheap, and if it is not, you have to make sure price is not their concern.

In large companies, technology enthusiasts can most often be found in the advanced technology group, or some such congregation, chartered with keeping the company abreast of the latest developments in high tech. There they are empowered to buy one of almost anything, simply to explore its properties and examine its usefulness to the corporation. In smaller companies, which do not have such budgetary luxuries, the technology enthusiast may well be the "designated techie" in the IT (information technology) group or a member of a product design team who either will specify your product for inclusion into the overall system or supply it to the rest of the team as a technology aid or tool.

To reach technology enthusiasts, you need to place your message in one of their various haunts—on the Web, of course.

Direct response advertising works well with this group, as they are the segment most likely to send for literature, or a free demo, a webinar, or whatever else of substance you offer. Just don't waste your money on a lot of fancy image advertising—they read all that as marketing hype. Direct email will reach them—and provided it is factual and new information, they read cover to cover.

In sum, technology enthusiasts are easy to do business with, provided you 1) have the latest and greatest technology, and 2) don't need to make much money. For any innovation, there will always be a small class of these enthusiasts who will want to try it out just to see if it works. That said, for the most part, these people are not powerful enough to dictate the buying decisions of others, nor do they represent a significant market in themselves. What they represent instead is a sounding board for initial product or service features and a test bed for introducing modifications to the product or service until it is thoroughly "debugged."

To give a prosaic example, in *In Search of Excellence* Tom Peters and Robert Waterman tell the story of the fellow at 3M who invented Post-it notes. He just put them on the desk of secretaries, and some of those secretaries just tried them to see if or how they would work. Those secretaries became Post-it note enthusiasts and were an early key in the campaign to keep the product idea alive.

Enthusiasts are like kindling: They help start the fire. They need to be cherished for that. The way to cherish them is to let them in on the secret, to let them play with the product and give you their feedback, and wherever appropriate, to implement the improvements they suggest and to let them know that you implemented them.

The other key to working with enthusiasts toward a success-ful marketing campaign is to find the ones who have access to the big boss. Big bosses are people who can dictate purchases and who do represent a significant marketing opportunity in and of themselves. To get more specific about the kind of big boss we are looking for, let us now turn to the next group in the Technology Adoption Life Cycle, the early adopters, or as they are often called in the high-tech industry, the visionaries.

Early Adopters: The Visionaries

Visionaries are that rare breed of people who have the insight to match up an emerging technology to a strategic opportunity, the temperament to translate that insight into a high-visibility, high-risk project, and the charisma to get the rest of their orga-nization to buy into that project. They are the early adopters of high-tech products. Often working with budgets in the multi-ple millions of dollars, they represent a hidden source of venture capital that funds high-technology business.

When John F. Kennedy launched the U.S. space program, he showed himself to be something we in America had not known for some time—a visionary president. When Henry Ford im-plemented factory-line mass production of automobiles so that every family in America could afford a car, he became one of our best-known business visionaries. When Steve Jobs took the Xerox PARC user interface out of the laboratory and put it into a Macintosh personal computer "for the rest of us," then drove the rest of the industry to accept this new approach in spite of itself, he showed himself to be a visionary to be reckoned with.

As a class, visionaries tend to be recent entrants to the ex-ecutive ranks, highly motivated, and driven by a "dream." The core of the dream is a business goal, not a technology goal, and it involves taking a quantum leap forward in how business is conducted in their industry or by their customers. It also involves a high degree of personal recognition and reward. Understand their dream, and you will understand how to market to them.

To give additional examples specific to high tech, when Harry McMahon at Merrill Lynch committed to put ten thousand people on Salesforce.com's cloud-based sales force automation system at a time when that vendor had no other large enterprise customer, he was acting as a visionary. When Linda Dillman at Wal-Mart committed to install Symbol RFID systems to create real-time visibility into all the inventory in every Wal-Mart store, she was acting as a visionary. When Reed Hastings, CEO of Netflix, committed to outsource the computing for his entire business to Amazon.com's Elastic Compute Cloud, he was acting as a visionary. And when Ted McConnell at Procter & Gamble committed to direct all digital advertising worldwide via AudienceScience's ad spend management system, he was acting as a visionary. In every case, these people took significant business risks with what at the time was unproven technology and/or an unproven company in order to achieve breakthrough improvements in productivity and customer service.

And that is the key point. Visionaries are not looking for an improvement; they are looking for a fundamental breakthrough. Technology is important only insomuch as it promises to deliver on this dream. If the dream is credit-card-free consumer purchasing, then it is likely to include e-wallets on a mobile device with near-field communication. If the goal is to provide elite education worldwide at no charge, then the technology will likely include MOOCs from institutions like Stanford University perhaps supplemented by material from an organization like the Khan Academy. If the goal is to provide virtually limitless mobile computing with highly infrequent refreshes of battery power, then it is likely to include a technology like Google Glass. If the goal is to provide personalized medicine where the drug is matched to your personal metabolism so that success rates are dramatically improved, then it will likely leverage molecular diagnostics from companies like CardioDx or Crescendo. The key point is that, in contrast with the technology enthusiast, a visionary focuses on value not from a system's technology per se but rather from the strategic leap forward such technology can enable.

Visionaries drive the high-tech industry because they see the potential for an "order-of-magnitude" return on investment and willingly take high risks to pursue that goal. They will work with vendors who have little or no funding, with products that start life as little more than a diagram on a whiteboard, and with technology gurus who bear a disconcerting resemblance to Rasputin. They know they are going outside the mainstream, and they accept that as part of the price you pay when trying to leapfrog the competition.

Because they see such vast potential for the technology they have in mind, they are the least price-sensitive of any segment of the technology adoption profile. They typically have budgets that let them allocate generous amounts toward the implementation of a strategic initiative. This means they can usually provide up-front money to seed additional development that supports their project—hence their importance as a source of high-tech development capital.

Finally, beyond fueling the industry with dollars, visionaries are also effective at alerting the business community to pertinent technology advances. Outgoing and ambitious as a group, they are usually more than willing to serve as highly visible references, thereby drawing the attention of the business press and additional customers to small fledgling enterprises.

As a buying group, visionaries are easy to sell but very hard to please. This is because they are buying a dream that, to some degree, will always be a dream. The "incarnation" of this dream will require the melding of numerous technologies, many of which will be immature or even nonexistent at the beginning of the project. The odds against everything falling into place without a hitch are astronomical. Nonetheless, both the buyer and the seller can build successfully on two key principles.

First, visionaries like a project orientation. They want to start out with a pilot project, which makes sense because they are "going where no man has gone before," and you are going there with them. This is followed by more project work, conducted in phases, with milestones, and the like. The visionaries' idea is to be able to stay very close to the development train to make sure it is going in the right direction and to be able to get off if they discover it is not going where they thought.

While reasonable from the customer's point of view, this project orientation is usually at odds with the intentions of entrepreneurial vendors who are trying to create a more universally applicable product around which they can build a multi-customer business. This is potentially a lose-lose situation threatening both the quality of the vendor's work and the fabric of the relationship, and it requires careful account management including frequent contact at the executive level.

The winning strategy is built around the entrepreneur being able to "productize" the deliverables from each phase of the visionary project. That is, whereas for the visionary the deliverables of phase one are only of marginal interest—proof of concept with some productivity improvement gained, but not "the vision"—these same deliverables, repackaged, can be a whole product to someone with less ambitious goals. For example, a company might be developing a comprehensive object-oriented software toolkit, capable of building systems that could model the entire workings of a manufacturing plant, thereby creating an order-of-magnitude improvement in scheduling and processing efficiency. The first deliverable of the toolkit might be a model of just one milling machine's operations and its environment. The visionary looks at that model as a milestone. But the vendor of that milling machine might look at the same model as a very desirable product extension and want to license it with only modest alterations. It is important, therefore, in creating the phases of the visionary's project to build in milestones that lend themselves to this sort of product spin-off.

The other key quality of visionaries is that they are in a hurry. They see the future in terms of windows of opportunity, and they see those windows closing. As a result, they tend to exert deadline pressures—the carrot of a big payment or the stick of a penalty clause—to drive the project faster. This plays into the classic weaknesses of entrepreneurs—lust after the big score and overconfidence in their ability to execute within any given time frame.

Here again, account management and executive restraint are crucial. The goal should be to package each of the phases such that each phase:

1. is accomplishable by mere mortals working in earth time
2. provides the vendor with a marketable product
3. provides the customer with a concrete return on investment that can be celebrated as a major step forward.

The last point is crucial. Getting closure with visionaries is next to impossible. Expectations derived from dreams simply cannot be met. This is not to devalue the dream, for without it there would be no directing force to drive progress of any sort. What is important is to celebrate continually the tangible and partial both as useful things in their own right and as heralds of the new order to come.

The most important principle stemming from all this is the emphasis on management of expectations. Because controlling expectations is so crucial, the only practical way to do business with visionaries is through a small, top-level direct sales force. At the front end of the sales cycle, you need such a group to understand the visionaries' goals and give them confidence that your company can step up to them. In the middle of the sales cycle, you need to be extremely flexible about commitments as you begin to adapt to the visionaries' agenda. At the end, you need to be very careful in negotiations, keeping the spark of the vision alive without committing to tasks that are unachievable within the time frame allotted. All this implies a mature and sophisticated representative working on your behalf.

In terms of prospecting for visionaries, they are not likely to have a particular job title, except that, to be truly useful, they must have achieved at least a senior vice presidential level in order to have the clout to fund their visions. In fact, in terms of communications, typically you don't find them, they find you. The way they find you, interestingly enough, is by maintaining relationships with technology enthusiasts. That is one of the reasons why it is so important to capture the technology enthusiast segment.

In sum, visionaries represent an opportunity early in a product's life cycle to generate a burst of revenue and gain exceptional visibility. The opportunity comes with a price tag—a highly demanding customer who will seek to influence your company's priorities directly and a high-risk project that could end in disappointment for all. But without this boost many high-tech products cannot make it to market, unable to gain the visibility they need within their window of opportunity, or unable to sustain their financial obligations while waiting for their marketplace to develop more slowly. Visionaries are the ones who give high-tech companies their first big break. It is hard to plan for them in marketing programs, but it is even harder to plan without them.

The Dynamics of Early Markets

To get an early market started requires an entrepreneurial company with a breakthrough technology product that enables a new and compelling application, a technology enthusiast who can evaluate and appreciate the superiority of the product over current alternatives, and a well-heeled visionary who can foresee an order-of-magnitude improvement from implementing the new application. When the market is unfolding as it should, the entrepreneurial company seeds the technology enthusiast community with early copies of its product while at the same time sharing its vision with the visionary executives. It then invites the visionary executives to check with the technology enthusiast of their choice to verify that the vision is indeed achievable. Out of these conversations comes a series of negotiations in which, for what seems like a very large amount of money at the time, but which will later be recognized as just the tip of the iceberg, the technology enthusiasts get to buy more toys than they have ever dreamed of, the entrepreneurial company commits itself to product modifications and system integration services it never intended to, and the visionary has what on paper looks to be an achievable project, but which is in fact a highly improbable dream.

That's when the market unfolds as it should. That is the good scenario—good because, although it is rife with problems, they are ones that will get solved one way or another, and some level of value will be achieved all around. There are numerous other scenarios where the early market does not even get a proper start. Here are some of them:

- First problem: The company simply has no expertise in bringing a product to market. It raises insufficient capital for the effort, hires inexperienced sales and marketing people, tries to sell the product through an inappropriate channel of distribution, promotes in the wrong places and in the wrong ways, and in general fouls things up.

  Remedying this kind of situation is not as hard as it may seem, provided the participants in the company are still communicating and cooperating with each other, and everyone is willing to scale back their expectations several notches.

  The basis for reform is the principle that winning at marketing more often than not means being the biggest fish in the pond. If we are very small, then we must search out a very small pond, a target market segment that fits our size. To qualify as a "real pond," as we also noted before, its members must be aware of themselves as a group, that is, it must constitute a self-referencing market segment, so that when we establish a leadership position with some of its members, they will get the word out—quickly and economically—to the rest.

Of course, no single pond of a size we can dominate in the short term is large enough to provide a sustaining market for the long term. Sooner or later, we have to expand into adjacent ponds. Or, to shift the metaphor, we need to reframe our tactics in the context of a "bowling pin" strategy, where one targets a given segment not just because one can "knock it over" but because, in so doing, it will help knock over the next target segment, and thus lead to market expansion. With the right kind of angle of attack, it is amazing how large and fast the chain reaction can be. So one is never necessarily out of the game, even when things are pretty bleak.

- A second problem: The company sells the visionary before it has the product. This is a version of the famous vaporware problem, based on preannouncing and premarketing a product that still has significant development hurdles to overcome. At best, the entrepreneurial company secures a few pilot projects, but as schedules continue to slip, the visionary's position in the organization weakens, and support for the project is eventually withdrawn, despite a lot of customized work, with no usable customer reference gained.

  Caught in this situation, the entrepreneurial company has only one adequate response, a truly unhappy one: shut down its marketing efforts, admit its mistakes to its investors, and focus all its energies into turning its pilot projects into something useful, first in terms of a deliverable to the customer, and ultimately in terms of a marketable product.

A company in the Mohr Davidow portfolio that did this brilliantly is Brickstream. Founded with artificial intelligence technology to extract information from video, it promised to give brick-and-mortar retailers the same kind of visibility into in-store traffic that e-tailers were getting from their clickstreams on the Web. Its first-generation systems were sold with great success, but implementation proved to be a bear, costs remained stubbornly and unacceptably high, and performance fell embarrassingly short. All those great sales turned into unreferenceable accounts, and it was dark days indeed.

Under a new management team the company has turned itself around dramatically. Its first act was to refocus on a much simpler problem—just counting the people that come into a store every day—and do that better, faster, and cheaper than the current technology. This had nothing like the dramatic impact they had been promising before, but it was a real business, and it was profitable. From there they eventually developed camera technology that could actually support their "brickstream" vision, and migrated into queue management at checkout counters, tying back into the workforce management needed to make sure staff was on hand at the right times of day. And most recently, they have incorporated additional camera technology and analytics to branch out further into security and inventory protection applications as well—all on the back of a prudently managed business that is cash-flow positive. To be sure, the company did lose its initial market window, but the good news is, the latest developments in retail and e-commerce are creating a second window to exploit.

- Problem number three: Marketing falls prey to the crack between the technology enthusiast and the visionary by failing to discover, or at least failing to articulate, the compelling application that provides the order-of-magnitude leap in benefits. A number of companies buy the product to test it out, but it never gets incorporated into a major system rollout, because the rewards never quite measure up to the risks. The resulting lack of revenue leads to folding the effort, either by shutting it down entirely or selling it for the technology assets to another enterprise.

The corrective response here begins with reevaluating what we have. If it is not, in fact, a breakthrough product, then it is never going to create an early market. But perhaps it could serve as a supplementary product in an existing mainstream market. If that is indeed the case, then the right response is to swallow our pride, reduce our financial expectations, and subordinate ourselves to an existing mainstream-market company, which can put our product in play through its existing channels. Computer Associates, today called CA Technologies and one of the largest software companies in the world, was built up almost entirely on this principle of remarketing other companies' often cast-off products.

Alternatively, if we truly have a breakthrough product but we are stalled in getting the early market moving, then we have to step down from the lofty theoretical plateau on which we have established that this product can be part of any number of exciting applications and get very practical about focusing on one application, making sure that it is indeed a compelling one for at least one visionary who is already familiar with us, and then committing to that visionary, in return for his or her support, to removing every obstacle to getting that application adopted.

These are some of the most common ways in which an early market development effort can go off—and be put back on—track. For the most part, the problems are solvable because there are always multiple options at the outset of anything. The biggest problem is typically overly ambitious expectations combined with undercapitalization—or, as my grandmother used to put it, when your eyes are bigger than your stomach. Things get a lot more complex when we are dealing with the dynamics of mainstream markets, to which we shall now turn.

Mainstream Markets

Mainstream markets in high tech look a lot like mainstream markets in any other industry, particularly where enterprises are selling to other enterprises. They are dominated by the early majority, who in high tech are best understood as pragmatists, who, in turn, tend to be accepted as leaders by the late majority, best thought of as conservatives, and rejected as leaders by the laggards, or skeptics. As in the previous chapter, we are going to look closely at how the psychographics of each of these groups influences the development and dynamics of a high-tech market.

Early Majority: The Pragmatists

Throughout the history of high tech, the early majority, or pragmatists, have represented the bulk of the market volume for any technology product. You can succeed with the visionaries, and you can thereby get a reputation for being a high flyer with a hot product, but that is not ultimately where the dollars are. Instead, those funds are in the hands of more prudent souls, who do not want to be pioneers ("Pioneers are people with arrows in their backs"), who never volunteer to be an early test site ("Let somebody else debug your product"), and who have learned the hard way that the "leading edge" of technology is all too often the "bleeding edge."

Who are the pragmatists? Actually, important as they are, they are hard to characterize because they do not have the visionary's penchant for drawing attention to themselves. They are not the Hamlets but the Horatios, not the Don Quixotes but the Sancho Panzas, in character more like Harry Potter than Dirty Harry—people who do not assert a position in life so much as derive one from what life provides. Never the standout, they are what makes for the continuity, so that after the star either dies (tragedy) or rides off into the sunset (heroic romance, comedy), they are left to clean up and to answer the inevitable final question: Who was that masked man?

In the realm of high tech, pragmatist CEOs are not common, and those there are, true to their type, tend to keep a relatively low profile. Dan Warmenhoven at NetApp, Jeff Weiner at LinkedIn, John Chen at Sybase, John Donahoe at eBay, even such visible leaders as Meg Whitman at HP and Michael Dell at Dell—low on drama, high on integrity and commitment. They tend to be best known by their closest colleagues, from whom they typically have earned the highest respect, and by their peers within their industry, where they show up near the top of the leaderboard year after year.

Of course, to market successfully to pragmatists, one does not have to be one—just understand their values and work to serve them. To look more closely into these values, if the goal of visionaries is to take a quantum leap forward, the goal of pragmatists is to make a percentage improvement—incremental, measurable, predictable progress. If they are installing a new product, they want to know how other people have fared with it. The word *risk* is a negative one in their vocabulary—it does not connote opportunity or excitement but rather the chance to waste money and time. They will undertake risks when required, but they first will put in place safety nets and manage the risks very closely.

The Fortune 2000 IT community, as a group, is led by people who are largely pragmatist in orientation. Business demands for increased productivity push them toward the front of the adoption life cycle, but natural prudence and budget restrictions keep them cautious. As individuals, pragmatists held back from using software-as-a-service applications until Salesforce.com made it safe to enter the water, held back from supporting bring-your-own-device policies until companies like MobileIron and Airwatch offered mobile device management solutions, and held back from investing in video until Cisco made *telepresence* a household word.

If pragmatists are hard to win over, they are loyal once won, often enforcing a company standard that requires the purchase of your product, and only your product, for a given requirement. This focus on standardization is, well, pragmatic, in that it simplifies internal service demands. But the secondary effects of this standardization on your growth and profitability—increasing sales volumes and lowering the cost of sales—is dramatic. Hence the importance of pragmatists as a market segment.

The most celebrated example and beneficiary of this effect in the last decade of the twentieth century was Microsoft. It created dominant market positions in desktop operating systems, office automation, and departmental servers, such that a decade later the enterprise landscape looked very homogeneous. At the same time, however, as each of these markets was developing, enterprise IT as a category also supported a variety of second-tier vendors, and each of these vendors was also able to carve out its own pragmatist enclave of its own. In the engineering community, customers gravitated to Sun's Solaris; in the graphics community, to Macintoshes; in the workgroup, to Novell Netware; in the Fortune 500 replicated-site environments of branch banking and retail, to OS/2; in the VAR-dominated professional services systems for doctors and dentists, to SCO Unix; and in consulting and financial services, to Lotus Notes. While Microsoft won out in the end, each one of these companies was able to ride a pragmatist wave within a specific market to boost its sales a quantum leap upward. It is crucial, therefore, for every long-term strategic marketing plan to understand the pragmatist buyers and to focus on winning their trust.

When pragmatists buy, they care about the company they are buying from, the quality of the product they are buying, the infrastructure of supporting products and system interfaces, and the reliability of the service they are going to get. In other words, they are planning on living with this decision personally for a long time to come. (By contrast, the visionaries are more likely to be planning on implementing the great new order and then using that as a springboard to their next great career step upward.) Because pragmatists are in it for the long haul, and because they control the bulk of the dollars in the marketplace, the rewards for building relationships of trust with them are very much worth the effort.

Pragmatists tend to be "vertically" oriented, meaning that they communicate more with others like themselves within their own industry than do technology enthusiasts and early adopters, who are more likely to communicate "horizontally" across industry boundaries in search of kindred spirits. This means it is very tough to break into a new industry selling to pragmatists. References and relationships are very important to these people, and there is a kind of catch-22 operating: Pragmatists won't buy from you until you are established, yet you can't get established until they buy from you. Obviously, this works to the disadvantage of start-ups and, conversely, to the great advantage of companies with established track records. On the other hand, once a start-up has earned its spurs with the pragmatist buyers within a given vertical market, they tend to be very loyal to it, and even go out of their way to help it succeed. At one time Salesforce.com was the disrupter in the sales force automation industry. Now it has become the de facto standard. When this happens, the cost of sales goes way down, and the leverage on incremental R&D to support any given customer goes way up. That's one of the reasons pragmatists make such a great market.

There is no one distribution channel preferred by pragmatists, but they do want to keep the sum total of their distribution relationships to a minimum. This allows them to maximize their buying leverage and maintain a few clear points of control should anything go wrong. In some cases this prejudice can be overcome if the pragmatist buyer knows a particular salesperson from a previous relationship. As a rule, however, the path into the pragmatist community is smoother if a smaller entrepreneurial vendor can develop an alliance with one of the already accepted vendors or if it can establish a value-added-reseller (VAR) sales base. VARs, if they truly specialize in the pragmatist's particular industry, and if they have a reputation for delivering quality work on time and within budget, represent an extremely attractive type of solution to a pragmatist. They can provide a "turnkey" answer to a problem, without impacting internal resources already overloaded with the burdens of ongoing system maintenance. What the pragmatist likes best about VARs is that they represent a single point of control, a single company to call if anything goes wrong.

One final characteristic of pragmatist buyers is that they like to see competition—in part to get costs down, in part to have the security of more than one alternative to fall back on should anything go wrong, and in part to assure themselves they are buying from a proven market leader. This last point is crucial: Pragmatists want to buy from proven market leaders because they know that third parties will design supporting products around a market-leading product. That is, market-leading products create an aftermarket that other vendors service. This radically reduces pragmatist customers' burden of support. By contrast, if they mistakenly choose a product that does not become the market leader, but rather one of the also-rans, then this highly valued aftermarket support does not develop, and they will be stuck making all the enhancements by themselves. Market leadership is crucial, therefore, to winning pragmatist customers.

Pragmatists are reasonably price-sensitive. They are willing to pay a modest premium for top quality or special services, but in the absence of any special differentiation, they want the best deal. That's because, having typically made a career commitment to their job and/or their company, they get measured year in and year out on what their operation has spent versus what it has returned to the corporation.

Overall, to market to pragmatists, you must be patient. You need to be conversant with the issues that dominate their particular business. You need to show up at the industry-specific conferences and trade shows they attend. You need to be mentioned in articles that run in the newsletters and blogs they read. You need to be installed in other companies in their industry. You need to have developed applications for your product that are specific to their industry. You need to have partnerships and alliances with the other vendors who serve their industry. You need to have earned a reputation for quality and service. In short, you need to make yourself over into the obvious supplier of choice.

This is a long-term agenda, requiring careful pacing, recurrent investment, and a mature management team. One of its biggest payoffs, on the other hand, is that it not only delivers the pragmatist element of the Technology Adoption Life Cycle but tees up the conservative element as well. Sadly, however, high-tech industry has, for the most part, not seen fit to reap the rewards it has so carefully sown. To see how this has come about, let us now take a closer look at the conservatives.

Late Majority: The Conservatives

The mathematics of the Technology Adoption Life Cycle model says that for every pragmatist there is a conservative. Put another way, conservatives represent approximately one-third of the total available customers within any given Technology Adoption Life Cycle. As a marketable segment, however, they are rarely developed as profitably as they could be, largely because high-tech companies are not, as a rule, in sympathy with them.

Conservatives, in essence, are against discontinuous innovations. They believe far more in tradition than in progress. And when they find something that works for them, they like to stick with it. Thus these folks are on Macs when everyone else is on Windows, then they are on Windows whenever everyone has switched back to Macs. They still use BlackBerrys, and they work just fine for them. They email rather than text and actually call each other from time to time. They neither tweet nor post, and their newspaper still arrives at the front door. And they are just fine with that, thank you very much.

In this sense, conservatives have more in common with early adopters than one might think. Both can be stubborn in their resistance to the call to conform that unites the pragmatist herd. To be sure, eventually conservatives do succumb to the new paradigm just to stay on par with the rest of the world. But just because they use such products doesn't mean they have to like them.

The truth is, conservatives often fear high tech a little bit. Therefore, they tend to invest only at the end of a technology life cycle, when products are extremely mature, market-share competition is driving low prices, and the products themselves can be treated as commodities. Often their real goal in buying high-tech products is simply not to get stung. Unfortunately, because they are engaging with the low-margin end of the market, where there is little motive for the seller to build a high-integrity relationship with the buyer, they often do get stung. This only reinforces their disillusion with high tech and resets the buying cycle at an even more cynical level.

If high-tech businesses are going to be successful over the long term, they must learn to break this vicious circle and establish a reasonable basis for conservatives to want to do business with them. They must understand that conservatives do not have high aspirations about their high-tech investments and hence will not support high price margins. Nonetheless, through sheer volume, they can offer great rewards to the companies that serve them appropriately.

Conservatives like to buy preassembled packages, with everything bundled, at a heavily discounted price. The last thing they want to hear is that the software they just bought doesn't support the home network they have installed. They want high-tech products to be like refrigerators—you open the door, the light comes on automatically, your food stays cold, and you don't have to think about it. The products they understand best are those dedicated to a single function—music, video, email, games. The notion that a single device could do all four of these functions does not excite them—instead, it is something they find vaguely nauseating.

The conservative marketplace provides a great opportunity, in this regard, to take low-cost, trailing-edge technology components and repackage them into single-function systems for specific business needs. The quality of the package should be quite high because there is nothing in it that has not already been thoroughly debugged. The price should be quite low because all the R&D has long since been amortized, and every bit of the manufacturing learning curve has been taken advantage of. It is, in short, not just a pure marketing ploy but a true solution for a new class of customer.

There are two keys to success here. The first is to have thoroughly thought through the "whole solution" to a particular target end-user market's needs, and to have provided for every element of that solution within the package. This is critical because there is no profit margin to support an after-purchase support system. The other key is to have lined up a low-overhead distribution channel that can get this package to the target market effectively. In this context, the rise of "as-a-service" offerings delivered over the Web creates a magnificent opportunity to make progress with this segment.

Conservatives represent a major opportunity for the high-tech industry in that they greatly extend the market for high-tech offers that are no longer state-of-the-art. The fact that the United States has all but conceded great hunks of this market to the Far East is testimony not so much to the cost advantages of offshore manufacturing as to the failure of onshore product planning and marketing imagination. Many offshore solutions today still bring only one value to the table—low cost. Conservatives are indeed price sensitive, but that is largely because they cannot get full value from their user experience. If you give them something they can relate to, they are more than willing to pay up for it. Just check out an Apple Store. Far more dollars could be mined from this segment of the high-tech marketplace if American leading-edge manufacturers and marketers, with their high-volume channels and vast purchasing resources, simply paid more attention to it.

So, the conservative market is still something that high tech has more in its future than in its past. The key is to focus on convenience rather than performance, user experience rather than feature sets. Backup cameras in cars are a great example of technology conservatives gravitate toward, as are parking assist systems. Even GPS applications have become more friend than foe. Not so, however, with speech-activated functions, for they lack the predictability that conservatives so desperately need.

Overall, one has the feeling that the conservative market is still perceived more as a burden than an opportunity. High-tech business success within it will require a new kind of marketing imagination linked to a less venturesome financial model. The dollars are there for the making if we can meet new challenges that are as yet only partially familiar. However, as the cost of R&D radically escalates, companies are going to have to amortize that cost across bigger and bigger markets, and this must inevitably lead to the long-ignored "back half" of the technology adoption curve.

The Dynamics of Mainstream Markets

Just as the visionaries drive the development of the early market, so do the pragmatists drive the development of the mainstream market. Winning their support is not only the point of entry but the key to long-term dominance. But having done so, you cannot take the market for granted.

To maintain leadership in a mainstream market, you must at least keep pace with the competition. At this point it is no longer necessary to be the technology leader, nor is it necessary to have the very best product. But the product must be good enough, and should a competitor make a major breakthrough, you have to make at least a catch-up response.

This is the game that Oracle has played masterfully in the first decade of the twenty-first century. After several decades of relying primarily on organic R&D to build out its portfolio of enterprise IT software, it changed the game when it made an unsolicited (and undesired) bid for PeopleSoft. When that acquisition finally closed, it inaugurated a new phase in enterprise IT, one of consolidation very much along the lines seen in earlier times for railroads, airlines, accounting firms, and more recently, banks. But in Oracle's case, it was not just bulking up in its traditional categories, but rather it was buying up the assets needed to create a top-to-bottom enterprise "stack," the full complement of what a Fortune 500 CIO would expect to own. This included customer relationship management from Seibel, application server middleware from BEA, and product life cycle management software from Agile, and eventually led even to annexing Sun Microsystems for a complete hardware solution as well.

Such consolidations are designed to conserve rather than to innovate. It is not that innovation has ceased but rather that it has relocated. Technologies from a prior era, once the focal point of innovation, now become the scaffolding upon which next-generation innovation will build. In that context, stability and predictability become much more highly valued, and ecosystems are willing to pay a premium to a core set of vendors to maintain them.

The key to making a smooth transition from the pragmatist to the conservative market segments is to maintain a strong relationship with the former, always giving them an open door to go to the new paradigm, while still keeping the latter happy by adding value to the old infrastructure. It is a balancing act to say the least, but properly managed, the earnings potential in loyal mature market segments is very high indeed.

In this regard, if we now look back over the first four profiles in the Technology Adoption Life Cycle, we see an interesting trend. The importance of the product itself, its unique functionality, when compared to the importance of the ancillary services to the customer, is at its highest with the technology enthusiast, and at its lowest with the conservative. This is no surprise, since one's level of involvement and competence with a high-tech product is a prime indicator of when one will enter the Technology

Adoption Life Cycle. The key lesson is that the longer your product is in the market, the more mature it becomes, and the more important the service element is to the customer. Conservatives, in particular, are extremely service oriented.

In the last decade, high tech has truly come to grips with this phenomenon by actively reconfiguring its product offers as services. Software as a service (SaaS), data center infrastructure as a service (IaaS), development and deployment platform software as a service (PaaS)—all are creating a new stack in the cloud, that virtualized space to which more and more computing is migrating.

To get to this place, two things have to happen in coordination with one another. The first is that vendors must design out as much as possible the service demands that derive from installing and implementing their products successfully. This is service-as-a-tax, adding no value, being simply the price you have to pay to get the stuff to work. This is still extraordinarily high for enterprise IT software, and while it has created a lot of income for systems integrators, it has left a bad taste in everyone's mouth, so the less of it, the better.

By contrast, when vendors address the second goal of making the service yield an improved user experience, then there are smiles all around. The Apple iPad is a wonderful example here, for it appeals not only to technology enthusiasts and visionaries ("It is just so cool!"), but equally so to pragmatists ("No training costs!") and to conservatives ("No training, period!"). When you watch a toddler playing with one, you realize just how far we have come from control-alt-delete.

That said, there will always be people who still feel disenfranchised by high tech, and it is to their issues that we will now turn.

Laggards: The Skeptics

Skeptics—the group that makes up the last one-sixth of the Technology Adoption Life Cycle—do not participate in the high-tech marketplace, except to block purchases. Thus, the primary function of high-tech marketing in relation to skeptics is to neutralize their influence. In a sense, this is a pity because skeptics can teach us a lot about what we are doing wrong—hence this postscript.

One of the favorite arguments of skeptics is that disruptive innovations of any kind rarely fulfill their promises and almost always come with unintended consequences. This combination of elusive reward with omnipresent risk just looks to them like a bad bet. Of course, visionaries and pragmatists are quite adept at overcoming these objections; otherwise there would be no high-tech industry for us to discuss. But what if, instead of rushing to rebuttal, we were to explore the merits of the skeptic's argument?

The point is, as any experienced seller of high-tech products can tell you, cost justification of high-tech purchases is a shaky venture at best. There is always the potential to return significant dollars, but it always depends on factors beyond the system itself. Put another way, this simply means that the claims that salespeople make for high-tech products are really claims made for "whole product solutions" that incorporate elements well beyond whatever high-tech manufacturers ship inside their boxes. If high-tech marketers do not take responsibility for seeing that the whole product solution is being delivered, then they are giving the skeptic an opening to block the sale. (For all the reasons just cited, the significance of whole product solutions is discussed at length later as the key component of successfully crossing the chasm and entering into the mainstream.)

What skeptics are struggling to point out is that new systems, for the most part, don't deliver on the promises that were made at the time of their purchase. This is not to say they do not end up delivering value, but rather that the value they actually deliver is not often anticipated at the time of purchase. If this is true—and to some degree I believe it is—it means that committing to a new system is a much greater act of faith than normally imagined. It means that the primary value in the act derives more from such notions as supporting a bias toward action than from any quantifiable packet of cost-justified benefits. The idea that the value of the system will be discovered rather than known at the time of installation implies, in turn, that product flexibility and adaptability, as well as ongoing account service, should be critical components of any buyer's evaluation checklist.

Ultimately the service that skeptics provide to high-tech marketers is to point continually to the discrepancies between the sales claims and the delivered product. These discrepancies, in turn, create opportunities for the customer to fail, and such failures, through word of mouth, will ultimately come back to haunt us as lost market share. Steamrolling over the skeptics, in other words, may be a great sales tactic, but it is a poor marketing one. From a marketing point of view, we are all subject to the "Emperor's New Clothes" syndrome, but particularly so in high tech, where every player in the market has a vested interest in boosting the overall perception of the industry. Skeptics don't buy our act. We ought to take advantage of that fact.

Back to the Chasm

As the preceding pages indicate, there is clearly a lot of value in the Technology Adoption Life Cycle as a marketing model. By isolating the psychographics of customers based on when they tend to enter the market, it gives clear guidance on how to develop a marketing program for an innovative product.

The basic flaw in the model, as we have said, is that it implies a smooth and continuous progression across segments over the life of a product, whereas experience teaches just the opposite. Indeed, making the marketing and communications transition between any two adoption segments is normally excruciatingly awkward because you must adopt new strategies just at the time you have become most comfortable with the old ones.

The biggest problem during this transition period is the lack of a customer base that can be referenced at the time of making the transition into a new segment. As we saw when we redrew the Technology Adoption Life Cycle, the spaces between segments indicate the credibility gap that arises from seeking to use the group on the left as a reference base to penetrate the segment on the right.

In some cases, the basic affinities of the market keep groups relatively close together. Early-adopting visionaries, for example, tend to keep in touch with and respect the views of technology enthusiasts; this is because they need the latter to serve as a reality check on the technical feasibility of their vision and to help evaluate specific products. As a result, enthusiasts can speak to at least some of the visionaries' concerns.

In a comparable way, conservatives look to pragmatists to help lead them in their technology purchases. Both groups like to see themselves as members of a particular industry first, businesspeople second, and purchasers of technology third. Pragmatists, however, have more confidence in technology as a potential benefit and in their ability to make sound technology purchases. Conservatives are considerably more nervous about both. They are willing to go along, up to a point, with pragmatists they respect, but they are still slightly unnerved by pragmatists' overall self-confidence. So, once again, the reference base has partial value in transitioning between adoption segments.

The significance of this weakening in the reference base traces back to the fundamental point made about markets in the introduction: Namely, that markets—particularly high-tech markets—are made up of people who reference each other during the buying decision. As we move from segment to segment in the technology adoption life cycle, we may have any number of references built up, but they may not be of the right sort.

Nowhere is this better seen than in the transition between visionaries and pragmatists. If there are to some extent minor gaps between the other adoption groups, between visionaries and pragmatists there is a great—and to a large extent, greatly ignored—chasm.

If we look deep into that chasm, we see four fundamental characteristics of visionaries that alienate pragmatists.

Visionaries lack respect for the value of colleagues' experiences. Visionaries are the first people in their industry segment to see the potential of the new technology. Fundamentally, they see themselves as smarter than their opposite numbers in competitive companies—and quite often they are. Indeed, it is their ability to see things first that they want to leverage into a competitive advantage. That advantage can only come about if no one else has discovered it. They do not expect, therefore, to be buying a well-tested product with an extensive list of industry references. Indeed, if such a reference base exists, it will almost certainly turn them off, indicating that for this technology, at any rate, they are already too late.

Pragmatists, on the other hand, deeply value the experience

of their colleagues in other companies. When they buy, they expect extensive references, and they want a good number to come from companies in their own industry segment. This, as we have already noted, creates a catch-22 situation; since there are usually only one or two visionaries per industry segment, how can you accumulate the number of references a pragmatist requires, when virtually everyone left to call on is also a pragmatist?

Visionaries take a greater interest in technology than in their industry. Visionaries are defining the future. You meet them at technology conferences and other futurist forums where people gather to forecast trends and seek out new market opportunities. They are easy to strike up a conversation with, and they understand and appreciate what high-tech companies and high-tech products are trying to do. They want to talk ideas with bright people. They are bored with the mundane details of their own industries. They like to talk and think high tech.

Pragmatists, on the other hand, don't put a lot of stake in futuristic things. They see themselves more in present-day terms, as the people devoted to making the wheels of their industry turn. Therefore, they tend to invest their convention time in industry-specific forums discussing industry-specific issues. Where pragmatists are concerned, sweeping changes and global advantages may make for fine speeches, but not much else.

Visionaries fail to acknowledge the importance of existing product infrastructure. Visionaries are building systems from the ground up. They are incarnating their vision. They do not expect to find components for these systems lying around. They do not expect standards to have been established— indeed, they are planning to set new standards. They do not expect support groups to be in place, procedures to have been established, or third parties to be available to share in the workload and the responsibility.

Pragmatists expect all these things. When they see visionaries forging their own paths with little or no thought of connecting with the mainstream practices in their industry, they shudder. Pragmatists have based their careers on such connections. Once again, it is painfully obvious that visionaries, as a group, make a very poor reference base for pragmatists.

Visionaries have little self-awareness about the impact of their disruptiveness. From a pragmatist's point of view, visionaries are the people who come in and soak up all the budget for their pet projects. If the project is a success, they take all the credit, while the pragmatists get stuck trying to maintain a system that is so "state-of-the-art" no one is quite sure how to keep it working. If the project fails, visionaries always seem to be a step ahead of the disaster, getting out of town while they can, and leaving the pragmatists to clean up the mess. Visionaries, successful or not, don't plan to stick around long. They see themselves on a fast track that has them leapfrogging up the corporate ladder and across corporations. Pragmatists, on the other hand, tend to be committed long term to their profession and the company at which they work. They are very cautious about grandiose schemes because they know they will have to live with the results.

All in all, it is easy to see why pragmatists are not anxious to reference visionaries in their buying decisions. Hence the chasm. This situation can be further complicated if the high-tech company, fresh from its marketing successes with visionaries, neglects to change its sales pitch. Thus, the company may be trumpeting its recent success at early test sites when what the pragmatist really wants to hear about are up-and-running production installations. Or the company may be saying "state-of-the-art" when the pragmatist wants to hear "industry standard."

The problem goes beyond pitches and positioning, though. It is fundamentally a problem of time. The high-tech vendor wants—indeed, needs—the pragmatist to buy now, and the pragmatist needs—or at least wants—to wait. Both have absolutely legitimate positions. The fact remains, however, that somewhere a clock has been started, and the question is, who is going to blink first?

For everyone's sake, it had better be the pragmatist. How to make sure of this outcome is the subject of the next section.

PART TWO

Crossing the Chasm

3

The D-Day Analogy

The chasm is, by any measure, a very bad place to be. It promises few, if any, new customers—only those who have somehow got off the safe thoroughfares. But it does house all sorts of unpleasant folk, from disenchanted current customers to nasty competitors to unsavory investors. Their efforts conspire to tax the reserves of the fledgling enterprise seeking to pass through to the mainstream. We need to look briefly at these challenges so we can be alert in our defenses against them.

The Perils of the Chasm

Let's begin with the lack of new customers. As opportunities from the early market of visionaries become increasingly saturated (with big-ticket products this can be after as few as three to five contracts), and with the mainstream market of pragmatists nowhere near the comfort level they need in order to buy, there is simply an insufficient marketplace of available dollars to sustain the firm. Having flirted with going cash-flow positive (especially during the months following one of the early market big orders), the trend is now reversed, and the enterprise is accelerating into increasingly negative cash flow. Worse still, mainstream competitors, who up to this time had paid no attention to the fledgling entry into their market, now have caught sight of a new target, experienced one or two major losses, and set their sales forces in motion to counterattack.

There are few opportunities for refuge. Managers would like to retreat into their existing major-account relationships, service them in an exceptional way, and leverage that investment of an additional year in fleshing out the greater part of the visionary's plan. This would not only ensure a secured reference base but also begin to create the infrastructure of ancillary products and interfaces needed to turn a discontinuous innovation into the pragmatist's idea of a real-world solution. Unfortunately, there are no extra dollars in these accounts to pay for this year. Indeed, this year of work is far more likely to be necessary just to catch up to the promises made to secure the deal in the first place. So, while there is plenty of good work to do, there is no additional money to pay for it.

Nor can managers find safety through continuing to service just the early market. To be sure, there are still sales opportunities here—other visionaries who can be sold to. But each one is going to have a unique dream, leading to unique demands for customization, which in turn will overtax an already burdened product development group. Moreover, sooner or later in this early market, yet another entrepreneur with a yet more innovative technology, and with a yet better story to tell, will come along. By then you have to be across the chasm and established in the mainstream, or you are out of luck.

There is still more peril. The marketing efforts to date have been funded by investors—either formally, as in the case of venture-funded enterprises, or informally, as is the case with new products developed within larger corporations. These investors have seen some early successes and now expect to see real progress against the business plan's long-term revenue growth objectives. As we now know, seeking this kind of growth during the chasm period is futile. Nonetheless, it is the commitment in the plan (if the commitment had not been made, the funding would not have been available) and the clock is ticking.

Indeed, a truly predatory type of investor—sometimes referred to as a *vulture capitalist*—looks to use the chasm period of struggle and failure as a means to discredit the current management, thereby driving down the equity value in the company, so that in the next round of funding, he or she has an opportunity to secure dominant control of the company, install a new management team, and, worst case, become the owner of a major technology asset, dirt cheap. This is an incredibly destructive exercise during which not only the baby and the bathwater but all human values and winning opportunities are thrown out the window. Nonetheless, it happens.

Even investors with reasonable demands and a supportive attitude, however, can be troubled by the chasm. Under the best-case scenario, you are asking them to rein back their expectations just when it seems most natural to let them fly. There is an underlying feeling that somehow, somewhere, someone has failed. They may be willing to give you the benefit of the doubt for a time, but you don't have any time to waste. You must get into a mainstream market segment soon, establishing long-term relationships with pragmatist buyers, for only through these can you control your own destiny.

Fighting Your Way into the Mainstream

To enter the mainstream market is an act of aggression. The companies who have already established relationships with your target customer will resent your intrusion and do everything they can to shut you out. The customers themselves will be suspicious of you as a new and untried player in their marketplace. No one wants your presence. You are an invader.

This is not a time to focus on being nice. As we have already said, the perils of the chasm make this a life-or-death situation for you. You must win entry to the mainstream, despite whatever resistance is posed. So, if we are going to be warlike, we might as well be so explicitly. For guidance, we are going to look back to an event in the first half of the twentieth century, the Allied invasion of Normandy on D-Day, June 6, 1944. While there may be more current examples of military success (although they do not spring to mind), this particular analogy relates to our specific concerns very well.

The comparison is straightforward enough. Our long-term goal is to enter and take control of a mainstream market (Western Europe) that is currently dominated by an entrenched competitor (the Axis). For our product to wrest the mainstream market from this competitor, we must assemble an invasion force comprising other products and companies (the Allies). By way of entry into this market, our immediate goal is to transition from an early market base (England) to a strategic target market segment in the mainstream (the beaches at Normandy). Separating us from our goal is the chasm (the English Channel). We are going to cross that chasm as fast as we can with an invasion force focused directly and exclusively on the point of attack (D-Day). Once we force the competitor out of our targeted niche markets (secure the beachhead), then we will move out to take over adjacent market segments (districts of France) on the way toward overall market domination (the liberation of Western Europe).

That's it. That's the strategy. Replicate D-Day, and win entry to the mainstream. Cross the chasm by targeting a very specific niche market where you can dominate from the outset, drive your competitors out of that market niche, and then use it as a base for broader operations. Concentrate an overwhelmingly superior force on a highly focused target. It worked in 1944 for the Allies, and it has worked since for any number of high-tech companies.

The key to the Normandy advantage, what allows the fledgling enterprise to win over pragmatist customers in advance of broader market acceptance, is focusing an overabundance of support into a confined market niche. By simplifying the initial challenge, the enterprise can efficiently develop a solid base of references, collateral, and internal procedures and documentation by virtue of a restricted set of market variables. The efficiency of the marketing process, at this point, is a function of the "boundedness" of the market segment being addressed. The more tightly bound it is, the easier it is to create and introduce messages into it, and the faster these messages travel by word of mouth.

Companies just starting out, as well as any marketing program operating with scarce resources, must operate in a tightly bound market to be competitive. Otherwise their "hot" marketing messages get diffused too quickly, the chain reaction of word-of-mouth communication dies out, and the sales force is back to selling "cold." This is a classic chasm symptom, as the entrepreneurial enterprise leaves behind the latent enthusiasm of the early market. It is usually interpreted as a letdown in the sales force or a cooling off in demand when, in fact, it is simply the consequence of trying to expand too rapidly and too broadly into too loosely bounded a market.

The D-Day strategy prevents this mistake. It has the ability to galvanize an entire enterprise by focusing it on a highly specific goal that is 1) readily achievable and 2) capable of being directly leveraged into long-term success. Most companies fail to cross the chasm because, confronted with the immensity of opportunity represented by a mainstream market, they lose their focus, chasing every opportunity that presents itself, but finding themselves unable to deliver a salable proposition to any true pragmatist buyer. The D-Day strategy keeps everyone on point—if we don't take Normandy, we don't have to worry about how we're going to take Paris. And by focusing our entire might on such a small territory, we greatly increase our odds of immediate success.

Unfortunately, sound as this strategy is, it is counterintuitive to the management of start-up enterprises, and thus, although widely acknowledged in theory, it is rarely put into practice. Here's the more common scenario:

How to Start a Fire

Starting a fire is a problem that any Boy Scout or Girl Scout can solve. You lay down some bunched-up newspaper, put on some kindling and some logs, and then light the paper. Nothing could be easier. *Trying to cross the chasm without taking a niche market approach is like trying to light a fire without kindling.*

The bunched-up paper represents your promotional budget, and the log, a major market opportunity. No matter how much paper you put under that log, if you don't have any target market segments to act as kindling, sooner or later, the paper will be all used up, and the log still won't be burning. When companies like Webvan, Solyndra, and Better Place burned their way through hundreds of millions of dollars in venture capital to absolutely no avail, this represented a very expensive lesson in scouting.

Starting a fire isn't rocket science, but it does represent a kind of discipline. And it is here that high-tech management shows itself most lacking. Most high-tech leaders, when it comes down to making marketing choices, will continue to shy away from making niche market commitments, regardless. Like marriage-averse bachelors, they may nod in all the right places and say all the right things, but they will not show up when the wedding bells chime. Why not?

First, let us understand that this is a failure of will, not of understanding. That is, it is not that these leaders need to learn about niche marketing. MBA marketing curricula of the past twenty-five years have been adamant about the need to segment markets and the advantages gained thereby. No one, therefore, can or does plead ignorance. Instead, the claim is made that, although niche strategy is generally best, we do not have time—or we cannot afford—to implement it now. This is a ruse, of course, the true answer being much simpler: *We do not have, nor are we willing to adopt, any discipline that would ever require us to stop pursuing any sale at any time for any reason.* We are, in other words, not a market-driven company; we are a sales-driven company.

Now, how bad can this really be? I mean, sales are good, right? Surely things can just work themselves out, and we will discover our market, albeit retroactively, led to it by our customers, yes? The true answers to the previous three questions are: 1) disastrous, 2) not always, and 3) never in a million years.

To put it simply, the consequences of being sales-driven during the chasm period are fatal. Here's why: The sole goal of the company during this stage of market development must be to secure a beachhead in a mainstream market—that is, to create a pragmatist customer base that is referenceable, people who can, in turn, gain us access to other mainstream prospects. To capture this reference base, we must ensure that our first set of customers completely satisfy their buying objectives. To do that, we must ensure that the customer gets not just the product but what we will describe in a later chapter as the whole product—the complete set of products and services needed to achieve their desired result, the thing we promised them to get the purchase order. Whenever anything is left out from this set, the solution is incomplete, the selling promise unfulfilled, and the customer unavailable for referencing. Therefore, to secure these much-needed references, which is our prime goal in crossing the chasm, we must commit ourselves to providing, or at least guaranteeing the provision of, the whole product.

Whole product commitments, however, are expensive. Even when we recruit partners and allies to help fulfill them, they require resource-intensive management. And when the support role falls back on us, it often requires the attention of our most key people, the same people who are critical to every other project we have going. Therefore, whole product commitments must be made not only sparingly but also strategically—that is, made with a view toward leveraging them over multiple sales. This can only happen if the sales effort is focused on a single niche market. More than one, and you take on additional use cases, causing you to burn out your key resources, falter on the quality of your whole product commitment, and prolong your stay in the chasm. To be truly sales-driven is to invite a permanent stay.

For reasons of whole product leverage alone, the sales-driven strategy should be avoided. But its siren lure is so strong that additional ammunition against it is warranted. Consider the following: One of the keys in breaking into a new market is to establish a strong word-of-mouth reputation among buyers. Numerous studies have shown that in the high-tech buying process, word of mouth is the number-one source of information that buyers reference, both at the beginning of the sales cycle, to establish their "long lists," and at the end, when they are paring down their short ones. Now, for word of mouth to develop in any particular marketplace, there must be a critical mass of informed individuals who meet from time to time and, in exchanging views, reinforce the product's or the company's positioning. That's how word of mouth spreads.

Seeding this communications process is expensive, particularly once you leave the early market, which in general can be reached through the technical press and related media. By contrast, pragmatist buyers, as we have already noted, communicate along industry lines or through professional associations. Chemists talk to other chemists, lawyers to other lawyers, insurance executives to other insurance executives, and so on. Winning over one or two customers in each of five or ten different segments—the consequence of taking a sales-driven approach—will create no word-of-mouth effect. Your customers may try to start a conversation about you, but there will be no one there to reinforce it. By contrast, winning four or five customers in one segment will create the desired effect. Thus, the segment-targeting company can expect word-of-mouth leverage early in its crossing-the-chasm marketing effort, whereas the sales-driven company will get it much later, if at all. This lack of word of mouth, in turn, makes selling the product that much harder, thereby adding to the cost and the unpredictability of sales.

Finally, there is a third compelling reason to be niche focused when crossing the chasm, which has to do with the need to achieve market leadership. Pragmatist customers want to buy from market leaders. Their motive is simple: Whole products grow up around the market-leading products and not around the others. That is, there are many more mobile apps for Apple and Android mobile devices than there are for Windows 8 or BlackBerry. There is a much broader base of talent to support Cisco routers and switches than Juniper's. The existence of this added-value infrastructure not only enriches the value of the product but also simplifies the task of getting support, at no additional cost to either the vendor or the customer.

Pragmatists are very much aware of this effect. As a result, perhaps unconsciously but nonetheless consistently, they conspire to install some company or product as the market leader and then do everything in their power to keep them there. One of the main reasons they delay their buying decisions at the beginning of a marketplace—thereby creating the chasm effect—is to help them get a fix on who the leader will be. They don't want to back the wrong one.

Now, by definition, when you are crossing the chasm, you are not a market leader. The question is, How can you accelerate achieving that state? This is a matter of simple mathematics. To be the leader in any given market, you need the largest market share—typically over 50 percent of the new sales at the beginning of a market, although it may end up to be as little as 30–35 percent later on. So, take the sales you expect to generate over any given time period—say the next two years—double that number, and that's the size of market you can expect to dominate. Actually, to be precise, that is the *maximum* size of market, because the calculation assumes that all your sales came from a single market segment. So, if we want market leadership early on—and we do, since we know pragmatists tend to buy from market leaders, and our number-one marketing goal is to achieve a pragmatist installed base that can be referenced—the *only right strategy is to take a "big fish, small pond" approach.*

Segment. Segment. Segment. One of the other benefits of this approach is that it leads directly to you "owning" a market. That is, you get installed by the pragmatists as the leader, and from then on, they conspire to help keep you there. This means that there are significant barriers to entry for any competitors, regardless of their size or the added features they have in their product. Mainstream customers will, to be sure, complain about your lack of features and insist you upgrade to meet the competition. But, in truth, mainstream customers like to be "owned"—it simplifies their buying decisions, improves the quality and lowers the cost of whole product ownership, and provides security that the vendor is here to stay. They demand attention, but they are on your side. As a result, an owned market can take on some of the characteristics of an annuity—a building block in good times, and a place of refuge in bad—with far more predictable revenues and far lower cost of sales than can otherwise be achieved.

For all these reasons—for whole product leverage, for word-of-mouth effectiveness, and for perceived market leadership—it is critical that, when crossing the chasm, you focus exclusively on achieving a dominant position in one or two narrowly bounded market segments. If you do not commit fully to this goal, the odds are overwhelmingly against your ever arriving in the mainstream market.

What About Microsoft?

Let me admit from the outset that, to the best of my knowledge, Microsoft has never followed the niche strategy that I have been so strongly advocating. It has not been a practitioner of the D-Day approach. Instead, it has continually taken what might be called the "Evel Knievel approach": Ignore the chasm. So how in the world has it been so successful, and why wouldn't anybody with a grain of sense follow their model, Mr. Moore, instead of yours?

Here I think we have an example of the legal profession's notion that great cases make bad law. Microsoft's history is so unique it makes it virtually unusable as a precedent for strategy decisions in other companies. Three of its primary technologies—Windows, NT, and Internet Explorer—have been direct extensions of a PC operating system franchise that Microsoft inherited and then stole from IBM.

That act of theft was Promethean—the stealing of fire from the gods and giving it to humans. It was not dishonest, it was brilliant. But the key point here is, Microsoft from day one was operating in a context of being a de facto standard. It was born inside a tornado of demand that IBM created, and all its subsequent acts of market development have been based on being the rich heir to that estate.

That status has allowed Microsoft to co-opt new technologies rather than have to introduce them directly. Its success, in other words, has been based primarily on being a fast follower of technologies introduced first by others. This is clearly true both for Windows, which was derived directly from the Macintosh, and the Internet Explorer, derived directly from Netscape Navigator. It is also clearly true of Office, whose anchor products (Word, PowerPoint, and Excel) all overtook established vendors (WordPerfect, Adobe, and Lotus), during the transition from DOS to Windows.

The point here is not to deride Microsoft's often alleged lack of innovation but rather to celebrate its market development strategy. As owner of all the clients in the client/server revolution of the 1990s, it had a permanent enclave on the pragmatist side of the chasm. It controlled the gates to the city. When barbarians showed up with their discontinuous innovations, it could shut the gates. When it showed up with its own versions of same, it could open the gates. They were Gates's gates, and the franchise was very lucrative indeed. It has taken the advent of mobile and cloud, disruptions more than a decade in the making, to put a dent in this position. But even now, Microsoft throws off cash flow that is the envy of anyone in the tech industry.

As spectacular a success as this is, nonetheless it is not a good precedent for the rest of us. Whereas Microsoft could (and perhaps still can) work both sides of the chasm simultaneously, most other companies have to cross without help. Indeed, often they have to cross in the teeth of Microsoft's resistance. Entering the mainstream market is an act of burglary, of breaking and entering, of deception, often even of stealth. Mapping out a global assault plan, attacking on all fronts at once, may work for massively intimidating market leaders who already have troops in place throughout the world, but it is just plain silly for stripling challengers. Instead, we need to pick our spots carefully, attack fiercely, and then dig in and hold.

Beyond Niches

Now, having said all that, we need also to acknowledge that there is life after niche. Major market dominance ultimately transcends niche, although it continues to renew and extend itself by developing new segments. And this is indeed when the truly large profits are made. It is clearly a post-chasm phenomenon, but there is a planning exercise to be done from the outset. Just as the *objective* of D-Day was to take Normandy beaches but the *goal* was to liberate Western Europe, so in our marketing strategy we want to establish a longer-term vision to guide our immediate tactical choices.

The key to moving beyond one's initial target niche is to select *strategic* target market segments to begin with. That is, target a segment that, by virtue of its other connections, creates an entry point into one or more adjacent segments. For example, when the Macintosh first crossed the chasm back in the 1980s, the target niche was the graphics arts departments in Fortune 500 companies. This was not a particularly large target market, but it was one that was responsible for a broken, mission-critical process—providing presentations for executives and marketing professionals. The fact that the segment was relatively small turned out to be good news because Apple was able to dominate it quickly and establish its proprietary system as a legitimate standard within the corporation (against the wishes of the IT department, which wanted everyone on an IBM PC).

More important, however, having dominated this niche, the company was then able to leverage its win into adjacent departments within the corporation—first marketing, then sales. The marketing people found that if they made their own presentations, they could update them on the way to the trade shows, and the salespeople found that with a Mac they didn't have to rely on the marketing people. At the same time, this beachhead in graphics arts also extended out into external markets that interfaced with the graphics arts people—creative agencies, advertising agencies, and eventually, publishers. All used the Macintosh to exchange a variety of graphic materials, and the result was a complete ecosystem standardized on the "nonstandard" platform.

How one goes about ensuring a strategic niche for the D-Day landing site is the subject of the next chapter. Before moving on to it, however, let's take a look at some highly visible companies who successfully implemented a highly focused approach to crossing the chasm.

Successful Chasm Crossings

In the discussions that follow we will look at three successful chasm crossings, each operating at a different level of "the stack" that makes up enterprise computing. The first example is Documentum, a content management database launched in the early 1990s, software that lives below the level that end users see, but above the systems software that governs servers and networks. This will be in contrast to our next two examples: Salesforce.com, whose initial flagship product very much is an end-user application, and VMware, whose flagship product is quite the opposite, being systems software that runs right on top of hardware and operating systems.

Why is this important? Well, software programs at the application layer are "naturally vertical" because they directly interface with end users, and end users organize themselves by geography, industry, and profession. This makes them readily adaptable to the beachhead focus needed to cross the chasm.

Later on in the life cycle, however, as solutions generalize, a horizontal approach is typically more productive, but this is a much harder challenge for an application offer to meet.

By contrast, infrastructure offerings have just the opposite dynamic. They are "naturally horizontal," because they interface with machines and other programs where the value, in part, is providing a stable, standard interface. They do not lend themselves to vertical marketing because, as products, they do not change very much from niche to niche.

Unfortunately, however, pragmatist customers rarely adopt any new technology en masse. Usually these innovations are taken up first by a single niche, one that has such pressing problems it goes ahead of the herd. The rest of the herd is delighted by this eventuality because it gets a free look at how well the technology plays out without having to take any immediate risk. The niche wins—presuming the beachhead strategy is conducted correctly—by getting a state-of-the-art fix for its heretofore unsolvable problem. And the vendor wins because it gets certified by at least one segment of pragmatists that its offering is legitimately mainstream.

So, *because of the dynamics of technology adoption, and not because of any niche properties in the product itself*, vendors of disruptive infrastructure must also take a vertical market approach to crossing the chasm even though it seems unnatural. The good news for them is that, later on, when a mass market emerges and horizontal marketing prevails, it is much easier to take advantage of the opportunity.

So to turn to our survey, we will start with what one might argue is the granddaddy of all chasm crossings, really the first great success of consciously applying the model, one that happened "back in the day" when client-server architecture was just becoming all the rage and no one was even talking about the Internet.

Documentum: A Document Management Application Crosses the Chasm

In 1993 when Jeff Miller took over the reins at Documentum, the company, despite inheriting a wealth of document management technology "for free" when it spun out of Xerox, had gone through three straight years of flat revenues in the $2 million range. This is a classic performance for a company whose market is in the chasm. In the year after Jeff came on board, it went to $8 million, then to $25 million, then $45 million (and an IPO), and then $75 million. That is world-class chasm crossing. What did Jeff and his team do?

Actually, they took the original edition of *Crossing the Chasm* and made it their market development blueprint. Knowing they were in the chasm, and knowing that the first key to getting out was to select a beachhead market segment, they surveyed their client experience to date and targeted a very thin market niche: the regulatory affairs departments in Fortune 500 pharmaceutical companies.

Now there are only about forty of these in the whole world, and the largest is a few dozen people or so, so how could a company justify reducing its market scope from "all personnel who touch complex documents in all large enterprises," to maybe one thousand people total on the planet?

The answer is that when you are picking a chasm-crossing

target it is not about the number of people involved, it is about the amount of pain they are causing. In the case of the pharmaceutical industry's regulatory affairs function, the pain was excruciating. This is the group that has to get the New Drug Approval applications submitted to the hundred or so different regulatory bodies around the world. The process does not start until patents are awarded. The patents have a seventeen-year life, and at the time Documentum was addressing the market, a successful patented drug generated on average about $400 million per year. Once the drug goes off patent, however, its economic returns plummet. Every day spent in the application process is a day of patent life wasted. Pharmaceutical companies were taking months to get their first application filed—not months to get it approved, months to get it submitted!

That was because new drug applications range from 250,000 to 500,000 pages in length, and come from a myriad of sources—clinical trial studies, correspondence, manufacturing databases, the Patent Office, research lab notebooks, and the like. All this material has to be frozen in time as a master copy, against which all subsequent changes in information are posted and tracked. It is a nightmare of a problem, and it was costing the drug companies big bucks—basically *one million dollars per day*!

By tackling this million-dollars-per-day problem, Documentum ensured itself a strongly committed customer. The commitment did not come from the IT organization, which *pragmatically* was content to work with its established vendors, making continuous improvements to the existing document management infrastructure. Instead, it came from the top brass, who, seeing in Documentum a chance to reengineer the entire process to a very different new end, overruled the in-house folks and demanded that they support the new paradigm.

This is a standard pattern in crossing the chasm. It is normally the departmental function who leads (they have the problem), the executive function who prioritizes (the problem is causing enterprise-wide grief), and the technical function that follows (they have to make the new stuff work while still maintaining all the old stuff).

In a year Documentum had demonstrated that it could solve this problem, and some thirty of the top forty pharmaceutical companies had committed to its solution. That is what drove its sales to $8 million and then to $25 million. But the revenue subsequent to that came from the bowling-pin effect of niche marketing.

Inside the drug companies, Documentum became the standard for all document management tasks, so it spread from the regulatory affairs group to the researchers to the manufacturing floor. Once it got to the floor, the plant construction and maintenance contractors, who were using it to assemble and maintain documentation on all the systems and procedures in the factory, recognized that factories in related process industries had the same needs, and they brought the product into regulated chemicals, nonregulated chemicals, and oil refineries. When the product hit the refineries, what people in the oil industry call the downstream part of their business, the IT people recognized a tool that could solve a major problem in their upstream business, exploration and production. There a key concern is the management of leasable properties, what options are available, what's under contract, who else is involved, et cetera. It is a rat's nest of interrelated contingencies, and without a document management system, it was being managed largely by word of mouth and paper files. Enter Documentum for another major success. And then that success caught the attention of Wall Street, who saw that the same facilities would help them get better control over their swaps and derivatives business. In the end, it turned out that financial services was the biggest customer segment for the company—but importantly, it was *not* the right target segment for crossing the chasm because its needs, while more pervasive, were not as urgent as those of the pharmaceutical industry.

And that is pretty much the chain of events that took Documentum to more than $100 million in revenues. It was niche marketing at its most leveraged. There are two keys to this entire sequence. The first is knocking over the head pin, taking the beachhead, crossing the chasm (and chaining together three mixed metaphors to do it!). The size of the first pin is not the issue, but the economic value of the problem it fixes is. The more serious the problem, the faster the target niche will pull you out of the chasm. Once out, your opportunities to expand into other niches are immensely increased because now, having one set of pragmatist customers solidly behind you, you are much less risky for others to back as a new vendor.

The second key is to have lined up other market segments into which you can leverage your initial niche solution. This allows you to reframe the financial gain in crossing the chasm. It is not just about the money you make from the first niche: It is the sum of that money plus the gains from all subsequent niches. It is a bowling alley estimate, not just a head pin estimate, that should drive the calculation of gain. This is a particularly important point for entrepreneurs working inside large corporations who are having to compete for funding against larger, more established market opportunities. If the executive council cannot see the extended market, if they only see the first niche, they won't fund. Conversely, if you go the other way, and show them only an aggregated mass market, the end result of the market going horizontal and into hypergrowth, they will fund, but then they will fire you as you fail to generate these spectacular numbers quickly. The bowling pin model allows you both to focus on the immediate market, keeping the burn rate down and the market development effort targeted, while still keeping in view the larger win.

Salesforce.com: A Software-as-a-Service Company Crosses the Chasm

From the very beginning of packaged enterprise applications, software was always delivered as a product to a client company's data center, where it was installed on their computers and integrated into their storage and networking systems. This required the client company to make significant investments both in capital equipment and operating budgets for expert staff. Moreover, it required significant systems integration efforts, typically costing several times more than the software itself, sometimes as much as ten times more. By the time the software was installed, there was often an updated release on the market, but the effort to put it in would be so great, customers normally forwent upgrade after upgrade, denying themselves all the latest innovations simply because the pain of adding them in was so great. There had to be a better way.

With the launch of Salesforce.com, CEO Marc Benioff announced to the world that there was indeed a better way, one that would spell the "end of software." It was called *software-as-a-service*, later to be abbreviated as SaaS, the idea being that there was one and only one copy of the software running at the vendor's data center, which multiple customers would use simultaneously, accessing it over the Internet. Each customer's data was kept isolated from every other customer's data, and the entire operation was secured by the latest technology managed by the most competent experts. Customers needed no data center, no expensive staff of IT professionals, and no systems integrators to get up and running on the system. To say the least, it was disruptive—not so much to the customer as to an entire application ecosystem that made its living off the old model.

You cannot threaten that many livelihoods without generating a backlash, and a backlash there was indeed. The enterprise ecosystem exclaimed that such a system was inherently insecure, that only a fool would put enterprise data "in the cloud." The PC ecosystem exclaimed that such an application was inherently dependent on the network, meaning unreliable response times and additional complexity above a packaged PC application running on an on-premise PC server. Skeptical analysts agreed that the idea was ahead of its time and dismissed it as yet another dot-com notion that was bound to flame out. Most doubted Salesforce would even get to the chasm, much less cross it. And yet, as it turned out, Salesforce has become the fastest-growing software company in history, approaching $4 billion in sales as of this writing, with growth rates north of 25 percent even at that size. So how did they do it?

Interestingly, they did not go after a vertical market. Instead they focused their segmentation along the following lines:

- They targeted salespeople and their managers only—not customer service, not marketing.
- They targeted mid-market companies, big enough to need systems to compete with market leaders in their category, small enough to be unable to afford the IT investment required.
- They focused on the United States only, in part to stay

close to the customer, in part because the United States has always been the early-adopting country in enterprise software.

- They focused on technology-savvy industries, beginning with high tech itself, then moving into telco, pharmaceuticals, and financial services.

The problem they were addressing was, quite simply, *making the quarter.* Unlike the incumbent sales automation packages, which were sold to enterprise executives to help them with budgeting and forecasting, Salesforce was designed first and foremost to help the salespeople themselves, giving them and their managers direct visibility into their pipelines, showing exactly what stage each prospect was in, alerting them to actions they could take to move it to the next stage. Unlike their competitors, which demanded significant effort to be kept up to date but gave little back in the way of day-to-day help, Salesforce was a true productivity tool.

Salespeople loved it—which was a first, believe me. And because they loved it, they told other salespeople about it, and adoption grew virally, not because some CIO had declared this was the new package, but because individual teams could sign up on their own without their CIO's help, or in some cases, without even his or her approval. Finally, because software-as-a-service is sold as a subscription, it was very much in Salesforce's interests to keep customers using the product, and since they ran the product themselves, they could see who was and who wasn't using it, and focus their support efforts accordingly. By contrast, while the packaged software vendors had sold all-you-can-eat enterprise-wide license agreements, many were in fact going unused, and no one was terribly incented to do anything about it. As a result, wherever Salesforce landed, it tended to expand, relatively unopposed.

A key lesson to learn here is that you want to target a beach-head segment that is:

- Big enough to matter
- Small enough to win, and a
- Good fit with your crown jewels.

That's what Salesforce did. By confining itself to the activities and the budgets of a single department, it was able to win more territory faster than if it had gone after a suite of applications crossing sales, service, and marketing. That would have required many more approvals and given the incumbents lots of chances to derail or at least slow down their growth. And because all their industries were U.S.-centered and "tech savvy," and because salespeople tend to job hop more than other professions, there was plenty of cross-pollination to help spread the demand virally.

There really wasn't much the incumbents could do to block them. All they could try really was to keep them out of the enterprise, which worked fine for a while, until Merrill Lynch caved and bought ten thousand seats, and then other financial services enterprises joined in the fray, and then the attack bloomed to full force. By that time, of course, the chasm was well in the rearview mirror.

VMware: Disruptive Infrastructure Crosses the Chasm

VMware makes software that "virtualizes" computers. What does that mean? Basically their software takes over a computer so that two different programs can run at the same time with each one in complete control of its own environment. It can also flip this idea by taking over two or more computers at the same time and making them look like a single great big one. Either way, applications do not see the actual computer but instead see a "virtual" computer, designed specifically for the purpose at hand.

Okay, but so what? Of course, that is precisely the question the world always asks of a disruptive innovation, and the sequence of unfolding answers follows the Technology Adoption Life Cycle. Here's how it played out in VMware's case.

The first use case adopted for VMware came from techies who wanted to be able to run both the Windows and the Linux operating systems on the same PC. This is something like wanting to run an automobile both on gasoline and compressed natural gas—unless you are a technology specialist, it is not likely you would be interested at all. But if you do write code, and at the same time are part of a larger organization, then you are quite likely to need your PC both for standard business applications (which typically run under Windows) and the technical applications you are developing (which typically run under some variant of Linux). In that case, being able to do all your work on one machine is a boon. So when VMware launched its first product for ninety-nine dollars, downloadable over the Internet, targeted at the PC aftermarket, it captured a strong position among technology enthusiasts.

The next two applications were more or less extensions of this same idea, creating a broader footprint for the same software, appealing still primarily to technologists. The first was to run two Windows applications on the same PC server. While in theory you did not need VMware to do this—Microsoft Windows itself supported the capability—in practice there were enough problems doing so that people just didn't. As a result, there were a whole lot of PC servers dedicated to running just one application, which can get expensive, especially when the second or third application is one you don't use all that often. VMware was designed to run two operating systems at the same time—so it did not care that both were actually the same. And it was robust enough that running two applications in tandem, the thing that created glitches for Windows, worked just fine. Score another small victory for the technologically astute.

And that led to another variation of this theme: running one application on two or more servers. Here the problem was that the application was getting so much use it was running out of room on a single server. The conventional answer was to buy a bigger server. The VMware answer was to use spare capacity from a second server—effectively for free. When budgets are flush, you might not worry about this. But in the years following the dot-com bust, IT departments were under increasing pressure to do more with less. Score another victory for VMware.

All these successes were pre-chasm, based on individuals applying technical know-how to solve corner-case problems. To cross the chasm you need a use case that poses equally challenging problems for the status quo solutions on a recurring basis. In the case of VMware its chasm-crossing use case showed up in the testing phase of the software development life cycle.

Think about it. You develop code semi-privately, and you can test for bugs on your own machine. But at some point you are going to want to run this thing in production, and before you do that, you will want to test it with a production load. You can't literally put it in production, so you have to spin up a shadow set of computers in parallel—and that's a lot of compute power. Moreover, you only want it for a relatively short period, after which you will put your program in production and will no longer need the test bench anymore. But this "spin up, spin down" approach is expensive—both in terms of getting the hardware and getting the system precisely configured to simulate your production environment accurately.

VMware came to the rescue. Not only could you reuse hardware you already had; you also could "save" your specialized testing environment so that you could load it back up in a jiffy. This meant a single hardware farm could simulate any number of production use cases, and it was available more or less upon demand. This was a huge win for systems administrators everywhere, and it was that use case that allowed VMware to cross the chasm.

Once it was across, additional use cases cascaded from this first one, subsequently allowing VMware to grow to the $5 billion company it is at the time of this writing. Once the systems administrator's needs had been handled, focus shifted to the IT operations manager. The word had gone out—we have to do more with less—how can we save money on hardware? Answer, "virtualize" the PCs we have. It turned out the unutilized capacity was staggering—as much as 90 percent! It was like someone backed up a truck and started unloading free PCs. Any wonder VMware grew like a weed during this period?

Later use cases got into reliability ("The email server never seems to go down anymore!"), making the VP of operations a much happier person, and agility ("This cloud thing is really cool!"), bringing a smile to the chief information officer's face. Virtualization, in sum, had become a pervasive computing strategy, a fundamental principle of provisioning servers across all applications. To be sure, this was well after the chasm had been crossed, but understand this was the dream from the very beginning. The key lesson for us here is that, despite the magnitude of this dream and its relevance to VPs of operations and CIOs everywhere, it was the lowly systems administrator with the niche market problem of simulating production environments for software testing who was the hero of our chasm-crossing venture.

From Idea to Implementation

The three previous examples illustrate the idea of crossing the chasm. Now it is time to move on to its actual implementation. In the next four chapters we will break up that challenge into four pieces. First we will look at how to select the point of attack, the place to cross, the beachhead, the head bowling pin. Then we will look at what kind of offer it will take to secure that initial target market, and how we as a fledgling enterprise with limited resources can go about fielding such an offer. Then we will look at the landscape, identifying the forces that seek to throw us off the beach and back into the chasm, and how we can position ourselves for success. And finally we will look at the selling systems themselves, pricing and distribution, to help us pick the right approach to the market during this particularly vulnerable time.

The critical attitude to maintain in all four of these challenges is that chasm crossing represents a unique time in your enterprise's history. It is a far cry both from your past, where selling to visionaries was the key to success, and your future, which will be focused on either niche or mass-market expansion programs. Between these two stages is a singular moment of transition, the penetration of the mainstream market, an act of burglary, of breaking and entering, that requires special techniques used at no other time in the Technology Adoption Life Cycle.

4

Target the Point of Attack

When it comes to crossing the chasm, Yogi Berra got it right:

> "If you don't know where you are going, you will wind up somewhere else."

The fundamental principle for crossing the chasm is to target a specific niche market as your point of attack and focus all your resources on achieving the dominant leadership position in that segment as quickly as possible. In one sense, this is a straight-forward market-entry problem, to which the correct approach is well-known. First you divide up the universe of possible customers into market segments. Then you evaluate each segment for its attractiveness. After the targets get narrowed down to a very small number, the "finalists," then you develop estimates of such factors as the market niches' size, their accessibility to distribution, and the degree to which they are well defended by competitors. Then you pick one and go after it. What's so hard?

The empirical answer here is, I don't know, but nobody seems to do it very well. That is, it is extremely rare that people come to the Chasm Group with a market segmentation strategy already in hand, and when they do have one, it is usually not one they are very confident about. Now, these are smart people, and a lot of them have been to business school, and they know all about market segmentation—so it is not for lack of intellect or knowledge that their market segmentation strategies suffer. Rather, they suffer from a built-in hesitancy and lack of confidence related to the paralyzing effects of having to make a *high-risk, low-data decision*.

A High-Risk, Low-Data Decision

Think about it. We already know that crossing the chasm is a high-risk endeavor, the effort of an unknown and unproven invasion force marching into the camp of some fierce and established competitor. We are either going to get it right, or we are going to lose a substantial portion, perhaps even all, of the equity value in our venture. In sum, there's a lot riding on this kind of decision, and severe punishment for making it badly.

Now, with that in mind, think about having to make what may be the most important marketing decision in the history of your enterprise *with little or no useful hard information*. For since we are trying to pick a target market segment that we have not yet penetrated to any great extent, by definition we also lack experience in that arena. Moreover, since we are introducing a discontinuous innovation into that market, no one has any direct experience with which to predict what will happen. The market we will enter, by definition, will not have experienced our type of product before. And the people who have experienced our product before, the visionaries, are so different in psychographic profile from our new target customers—the pragmatists—that we must be very careful about extrapolating our results to date. We are, in other words, in a high-risk, low-data state.

If you now turn to the established case studies in market segmentation, like as not you will discover they will be based on work done on market share problems *in existing markets*—in other words, work done in situations where there is already a considerable amount of data to work with. There are precious few paradigms for how to proceed when you cannot examine market share data, indeed cannot even conduct an informed interview with an existing customer of the type you are now seeking to win over. In short, you are on your own.

Now, the biggest mistake one can make in this state is to turn to numeric information as a source of refuge or reassurance. We all know about lies, damned lies, and statistics, but for numeric marketing data we need to open up a whole new class of prevarication. This stuff is like sausage—your appetite for it lessens considerably once you know how it is made. In particular, the kind of market-size forecasts that come out of even the most highly respected firms—the ones that get quoted in the press as showing the bright and promising future for some new technology or product—are, by necessity, rooted in multiple assumptions. Each of these assumptions has enormous impact on the resulting projection, each represents an experienced but nonetheless arbitrary judgment of a particular market analyst, and all are typically well documented in the report, but also typically ignored by anyone who quotes from it. And once a number gets quoted in the press, then God help us—because it has become *real*. You know it is real because pretty soon you see new numbers cropping up, with claims for their legitimacy based on their being derivations of these other "established" numbers.

As you can see, this whole thing is a house of cards. In some contexts, it even has some uses, particularly where financial managers must deal on a macro level with high-tech markets. But it is absolute folly to use such numbers for developing crossing-the-chasm marketing strategies. That would be like using a map of the world to find your way from the San Francisco airport to the Ferry Plaza.

And yet, that is what some people try to do. As soon as the numbers get up in a chart—or better yet, a graph—as soon as they thus become blessed with some specious authenticity, they become the drivers in high-risk, low-data situations because these people are so anxious to have data. That's when you hear them saying things like "It will be a billion-dollar market in 2016. If we only get five percent of that market . . ." When you hear that sort of stuff, exit gracefully, holding on to your wallet.

Now, most of the people who come to the Chasm Group are more sophisticated than this. They know the numbers do not provide the answers they need. But that doesn't mean they feel any better about having to make a high-risk, low-data decision—which means, in effect, they are stymied. It is our job to get them out of this semi-paralyzed state and back into action.

The only proper response to this situation is to acknowledge the lack of data as a condition of the process. To be sure, you can fight back against this ignorance by gathering highly focused data yourself. But you cannot expect to transform a low-data situation into a high-data situation quickly. And given that you must act quickly, you need to approach the decision from a different vantage point. You need to understand that *informed intuition*, rather than *analytical reason*, is the most trustworthy decision-making tool to use.

Informed Intuition

Despite our culture's anxiety about relying on nonverbal processes, there are situations in which it is simply more effective to substitute right-brain tactics for left-brain ones. Ask any great athlete, or artist, or charismatic leader—ask any great decision maker. All of them describe a similar process, in which analytical and rational means are used extensively both in preparation for and in review of a central moment of performance. But in the moment itself, the actual decisions are made intuitively. The question is, How can we use this testimony to our advantage in crossing the chasm in a reasonable and predictable way?

The key is to understand how intuition—specifically, *informed intuition*—actually works. Unlike numerical analysis, it does not rely on processing a statistically significant sample of data in order to achieve a given level of confidence. Rather, it involves conclusions based on isolating a few high-quality images—really, data fragments—that it takes to be archetypes of a broader and more complex reality. These images simply stand out from the swarm of mental material that rattles around in our heads. They are the ones that are memorable. So the first rule of working with an image is: If you can't remember it, don't try, because it's not worth it. Or, to put this in the positive form: Only work with memorable images.

Now, just as in literature, where memorable characters like Hamlet or Heathcliff or Dumbledore or Voldemort stand out and become symbols for a larger segment of humanity, so in marketing can whole target populations become imagined as Gen X, Gen Y, Goths, geeks, Beibers, Dinks (Double Income, No Kids), or Henrys (High Earners, Not Rich Yet). These are all just images—stand-ins for a greater reality—picked out from a much larger set of candidate images on the grounds that they really "click" with the sum total of an informed person's experience. Each is in effect a "poster child."

Let us call these poster children *characterizations* because they represent characteristic market behaviors. "Beibers," for example, can be expected to shop at a mall, emulate a rock star, seek peer approval, and resist parental restrictions—all of which imply that certain marketing tactics will be more successful than others in winning their dollars. Now, *visionaries*, *pragmatists*, and *conservatives* represent a set of images analogous to Goth or geek—albeit at a higher level of abstraction. For each of these labels also represents characteristic market behaviors—specifically, in relation to adopting a discontinuous innovation—from which we can predict the success or failure of marketing tactics. The problem is, they are too abstract. They need to become more concrete, more target market specific. That is the function of *target customer characterization*.

Target Customer Characterization: The Use of Scenarios

First, please note that we are not focusing here on target market characterization. The place where most crossing-the-chasm marketing segmentation efforts get into trouble is at the beginning, when they focus on a target market or target segment instead of on a *target customer*.

Markets as categories are impersonal, abstract things: the smartphone market, the gigabit router market, the office automation market, and so on. Neither the names nor the descriptions of markets evoke any memorable images—they do not elicit the cooperation of one's intuitive faculties. In fact, these are not "markets" at all in our sense of the term—they do not refer to populations of customers, but rather sets of competitors.

We need to work with something that gives more clues about how to proceed in the presence of real people with complex motives. However, since we do not have real live customers as yet—or at least, not very many of them—we are just going to have to make them up. Then, once we have their images in mind, we can let them guide us to developing a truly responsive approach to their needs.

Target customer characterization is a formal process for making up these images, getting them out of individual heads and in front of a market development decision-making group. The idea is to create as many characterizations as possible, one for each different type of customer and application for the product. (It turns out that, as these start to accumulate, they begin to resemble one another so that, somewhere between twenty and fifty, you realize you are just repeating the same formulas with minor tweaks, and that in fact you have outlined eight to ten distinct alternatives.) Once we have built a basic library of possible target customer profiles, we can then apply a set of techniques to reduce these "data" into a prioritized list of desirable target market segment opportunities. The quotation marks around *data* are key, of course, because we are still operating in a low-data situation. We just have a better set of *material* to work with.

3-D Printing: An Illustrative Example

For the purposes of illustration, let us consider how we might market a 3-D printer. At the time of this writing, they are getting a ton of attention in the press, so there is certainly an early market for them. Basically, you input a 3-D CAD file of the object you want, and the machine builds one up by manipulating a stream of polymer or laying down successive layers of a substrate. All sorts of artifacts have been prototyped, everything from toys, jewelry, and artworks to medical prostheses and industrial molds, and the variety and delicacy of the resultant shapes are pretty amazing.

Now, let us suppose that in the next few years 3-D printers continue to win over an early market of technology enthusiasts ("Hey, wanna see this cool pair of flip-flops I made yesterday?") and visionaries ("With 3-D printing, we can change the way eyeglass frame manufacturing is conducted—instead of make and then distribute, we can distribute and then make! Just think of the reductions in inventory and the opportunities to mass customize!"). Invisalign, the leader in next-generation orthodontia, has standardized on these methods to create their appliances, and they are revolutionizing the industry. Industrial manufacturers serving the major OEMs are using them for rapid prototyping, just to make sure they get the tooling right before they kick off mass production. And Tom Cruise puts a 3-D printer in his next movie, manufacturing a plastic gun that cannot be detected by conventional screening. Now it is time to go after the mainstream market, taking market share away from traditionally manufactured products. Where would you begin?

This is a classic case of "So many segments, so little time"— exactly the sort of thing that target customer scenarios are best for. A representative format for any given scenario is illustrated in the following section. A finished scenario should be limited to a single page. As you will see from the example, this is a highly tactical exercise in microcosm, but it has major implications for how marketing strategy is set overall. So as we work through the example, we will also keep an eye out for the broader implications.

Sample Scenario

1. **HEADER INFORMATION**. At the top of the page you need thumbnail information about the end user, the technical buyer, and the economic buyer of the offer. For business markets, the key data are: industry, geography, department, and job title. For consumer markets, they are demographic: age, sex, economic status, social group.

For our sample scenario, we are going to focus on a lighting designer who is bringing to market a new line of fixtures for the home. The plan is to sell these through wholesale distributors to interior decorators and designers acting as agents for their relatively wealthy clientele. In this context our key header information is:

Economic buyer: The client who ultimately pays for the lighting fixture.
End user: The interior designer who will guide the client in making the choice.
Technical buyer: The home maintenance provider or building contractor who will install the fixture.

Note: In off-the-shelf consumer scenarios, the three roles of user, technical buyer, and economic buyer tend to merge into one or two. If the user is a child, the economic buyer is the parent, and the technical buyer is a toss-up (in our house, the child for sure). If the user is an adult, the economic buyer often is the other spouse (as in, is it okay for me to spend our money on this doodad?), and the technical buyer tends to be the user. One caveat, though: It is extremely difficult to cross the chasm in a consumer market. Almost all successful crossings happen in business markets, where the economic and technical resources can absorb the challenges of an immature product and service offering. Alternatively, consumer markets can spin up with no chasms at all if the technology is already adopted and the disruption is coming from a new business model. (For an alternative market development model that describes these dynamics, see "The Four Gears" discussion in Appendix 2.)

Getting back to our scenario process, which is a B-to-B-to-C value chain, where both the distributor and the designer are intermediaries between the manufacturer and the consumer, the idea behind the header information is to focus the marketing and R&D teams on a specific instance of how the product would be bought and used. This is called a *use case*. Do not worry about being overly focused at this point—indeed, the more specific, the better. The devil is always in the details, and these scenarios are all about getting the devil in view.

2. A DAY IN THE LIFE (BEFORE) The idea here is to describe a situation in which the user is stuck, with significant consequences for the economic buyer. The elements you need to capture are five:

- *Scene or situation*: Focus on the moment of frustration. What is going on? What is the user about to attempt?
- *Desired outcome*: What is the user trying to accomplish? Why is this important?

- *Attempted approach*: Without the new product, how does the user go about the task?
- *Interfering factors*: What goes wrong? How and why does it go wrong?
- *Economic consequences*: So what? What is the impact of the user failing to accomplish the task productively?

Using lighting fixtures as an example, we might generate the following:

Scene or situation: David T is an interior designer with a wealthy but highly demanding client who wants "the perfect" fixtures for her remodeled living and dining area. David too has very high standards for such things, and the pair of them are determined to find something truly special.

Desired outcome: Locate and purchase lighting fixtures that enhance and extend the design themes of the two rooms. The goal is to combine a striking shape with simple lines and subtle colors, varying a single theme across several different fixtures. This will require a single designer to come up with multiple designs of different sizes and scale utilizing a common set of materials.

Attempted approach: David has been scouring the Design District for days, going to all his most reliable sources, gathering images and catalogs galore. He has reviewed these with his client, leading to an increasingly more precise sense of what they are looking for, but regrettably not finding it. A couple of close calls turned out to be unsuitable once they had gone to see them on display.

Interfering factors: The problem with the whole approach is that both David and his client would like to "co-design" the fixtures so they integrate perfectly with the other design themes in the home. Unfortunately, fixtures come already designed, and the entire industry is based on selecting from what is available. Moreover, the amount of inventory that would have to be displayed in order to represent a complete selection is prohibitively expensive, which means many catalog items end up having to be bought sight unseen (and then returned if found unsatisfactory). This is, of course, the perennial challenge of a retail merchandising model.

Economic consequences: David's client is not happy, which means David is not happy. It looks like they are going to end up having to settle for something that is okay but not "perfect," thereby undermining David's fundamental brand promise and the client's confidence in his ability to deliver on it. Moreover, the wholesaler who gets the business does not achieve the kind of customer loyalty he wants from David because he too is part of this chain of compromise as well.

3. A DAY IN THE LIFE (AFTER) Now the idea is to take on the exact same situation, along with the exact same desired outcome, but to replay the scenario with the new technology in place. Here you need to capture just three elements:

- *New approach:* With the new product how does the end user go about the task?
- *Enabling factors:* What is it about the new approach that allows the user to get unstuck and be productive?
- *Economic rewards:* What are the costs avoided or benefits gained?

Staying with the lighting fixtures example, we might generate the following:

New approach: David and his client have been reviewing catalogs and images over the Web for the better part of a week, and they have finally settled on a design. This is a variation on a couple of actual products that have been sketched out by David with input from the client. They take this design to a fixture wholesaler who supports 3-D printing. The wholesaler works with a freelance designer who is able to scan David's drawing and convert it into a CAD file. At the same time, the wholesaler works with David to select an appropriate material and finish for the fabricated fixture. Then both the CAD file and the material are fed into the printer, and out comes a finished fixture. If the client still wants to tweak it some more, this can be readily done by updating the file and printing it out again. Further, by adjusting the parameters in the file, fixtures of different scales can be produced, all sharing the same design.

Enabling factors: Three-D printers are able to manufacture upon demand. This eliminates both the expense and the compromise of having to select from premanufactured inventory. They have exceptional flexibility because their two key inputs—CAD files and printing material—are both readily modifiable to meet a wide variety of design requirements. CAD software systems running on ordinary PCs are now sufficiently powerful that they can adapt designs readily, and the 3-D printers, priced in the same range as PCs, are sufficiently fast to produce the artifacts in a matter of a few hours.

Economic rewards: David's client is thrilled with the result. Not only does she gladly pay the mark-up on the fixtures; she is also happy to pay his consulting designer fee. In fact, she is thinking about redoing the fixtures in the rest of the home. The wholesaler is delighted to have produced a showcase result, not to mention relieved not to have to carry a large inventory of product to support a relatively small stream of actual sales. The lighting fixture manufacturers meanwhile are seeing the writing on the wall and are beginning to publish designs suitable for 3-D printing. These will have lower prices, to be sure, but much higher margins, so they hope at the end of the day to make more money on less capital than in the past. And because the designs are just software, it is much easier to display them virtually over the Web, cutting out the need to man booths at expensive trade shows.

Processing the Scenario: The Market Development Strategy Checklist

Target customer characterization is at the core of applying market segmentation strategy to the problem of crossing the chasm. It supplies the "data." Assume that we have spent a day with a group of ten or so field-savvy members of the 3-D printing company compiling a library of, say, twenty to forty of these scenarios. In this library we have captured actual use cases from every current customer, every interesting prospect whether won, lost, or in waiting, as well as other interesting prospects that we might know about from past lives.

This is not a formal segmentation survey—they take too long, and their output is too dry. Instead, it is a tapping into the fund of anecdotes that actually carries business knowledge in our culture. Like much that is anecdotal, these scenarios will incorporate fictions, falsehoods, prejudices, and the like. Nonetheless, they are by far the most useful and most accurate form of data to work with at this stage in the segmentation process. Compared to SIC codes, for example, they are paragons of accuracy and integrity. Nonetheless, they are still crude at best, and now it is time to submit them to a refinery—the Market Development Strategy Checklist.

This list consists of a set of issues around which go-to-market plans are built, each of which incorporates a chasm-crossing factor, as follows:

- Target customer
- Compelling reason to buy
- Whole product
- Partners and allies
- Distribution
- Pricing
- Competition
- Positioning
- Next target customer

Processing the scenarios consists of rating each scenario against each of these factors. The process actually takes place in two stages. In Stage 1, all scenarios are rated against four "showstopper" issues. Low scores in any one of these typically eliminates the scenario from future consideration *as the beachhead segment*. That is, the niche may be a good one to pursue after the chasm has been crossed, but it is not a good target for the crossing itself.

Scenarios that pass the first cut are rated against the remaining five factors. At both stages scores are awarded for each factor, and the scenarios are rank ordered by score. At the end of the process, top-ranked scenarios are taken to be the top chasm-crossing targets. They are further discussed until the team commits to one—and *only* one—beachhead target.

The italics immediately above are meant to answer the single most asked question of the Chasm Group: *Can't we go after more than one target?* The simple answer is no. (The more complex answer is also no, but it takes longer to explain.) Just as you cannot hit two balls with one bat swing, hit two birds with one stone, or brush your teeth and your hair at the same time, so you cannot cross the chasm in two places. We've already discussed this, of course, but trust me, one cannot make this point too often.

Turning back to the checklist, the four factors that raise showstopper issues for crossing the chasm are as follows:

TARGET CUSTOMER: Is there a single, identifiable economic buyer for this offer, readily accessible to the sales channel we intend to use, and sufficiently well funded to pay the price for the whole product? In the absence of such a buyer, sales forces waste valuable time evangelizing groups of people trying to generate a sponsor. Sales cycles drag on forever, and the project can be shut down at any time.

COMPELLING REASON TO BUY: Are the economic consequences sufficient to make any reasonable economic buyer anxious to fix the problem called out in the scenario? If pragmatists can live with the problem for another year, they will. But they will continue to be interested in learning more. So your salespeople will be invited back again and again—they just won't return with any purchase orders. Instead, they will report that the customer said, "Great presentation!" What the customer was really saying was "I learned some more and I didn't have to buy anything."

WHOLE PRODUCT: Can our company with the help of partners and allies field a complete solution to the target customer's compelling reason to buy in the next three months such that we can be in the market by the end of next quarter and be dominating the market within twelve months thereafter? The clock is ticking. We need to cross now, which means we need a problem we can solve now. Any thread left hanging could be the one that trips us up.

COMPETITION: Has this problem already been addressed by another company such that they have crossed the chasm ahead of us and occupied the space we would be targeting? Dick Hackborn, the HP executive who led the move into laser printers, had a favorite saying: "Never attack a fortified hill." Same with beachheads. If some other company got there before you, all the market dynamics that you are seeking to make work in your favor are already working in its favor. Don't go there.

When scenarios are scored against these four factors, 1 to 5, the worst aggregate score they can get is 4, the best 20, with higher-rated scenarios preferred. But there is an additional caveat. A very low score, relative to the others, in any of these factors almost always is a showstopper. So it is not just total score alone that matters. When in doubt, favor scenarios that have a high-rated compelling reason to buy. If they have already attracted a competitor, see if you can't end-run them. Expect that the best scenarios will be "whole product challenged"—if it were easy, someone else would have done it. Indeed, the fact that it is hard will create a barrier to entry in your favor once you have stepped up to the solution.

The remaining factors fall into the "nice to have" category. That is, low scores can usually be overcome, given investment and time. Since, however, investment and time are two of your scarcest resources, cheaper and sooner are very desirable attributes in a target market scenario. Here's how they play out:

PARTNERS AND ALLIES: Do we already have relationships begun with the other companies needed to fulfill the whole product? If you do, it is typically from a single early-market project, or else you are just lucky. Pulling together this partnership is a major challenge for the whole product manager.

DISTRIBUTION: Do we have a sales channel in place that can call on the target customer and fulfill the whole product requirements put on distribution?

Calling on the line-of-business side of the house requires some fluency in the language of the target niche, and established relationships with targeted buyers and users accelerates this process dramatically. Lacking this, companies typically hire a well-connected individual out of the target industry and charter her to lead the sales force back in.

PRICING: Is the price of the whole product consistent with the target customer's budget and with the value gained by fixing the broken process? Do all the partners, including the distribution channel, get compensated sufficiently to keep their attention and loyalty?

Note here that it is the whole product price, not the price of the product per se, that matters. Services will often make up as much or more of this total as product.

POSITIONING: Is the company credible as a provider of products and services to the target niche?

At the outset, the answer is typically, Not very. One of the delights of niche marketing, however, is the speed at which this resistance can be overcome if only one truly commits to a whole product that fixes the broken process.

NEXT TARGET CUSTOMER: If we are successful in dominating this niche, does it have good "bowling pin" potential? That is, will these customers and partners facilitate our entry into adjacent niches?

This is an important issue of strategy. Chasm crossing is not the end, but rather the beginning, of mainstream market development. It is important that we have additional follow-on niches that can be lucratively addressed. Otherwise the economics of niche marketing simply do not hold up.

After the scenarios that passed the first round of showstopper screening have been scored on this second set of factors and then rank ordered by score, the team has extracted all of the "data" this process can provide. It is now time to make the high-risk, low-data decision and get on with it.

Committing to the Point of Attack

Making the commitment to a niche market can be challenging, especially for entrepreneurs who are technology enthusiasts or visionaries, because they personally don't have the pragmatist response and thus have trouble trusting in the market dynamics outlined in this book. This is a defining moment for them. The start-up company must either cross or die, but what value is life if to gain it one has to go against one's best self? Not an easy question to answer.

When faced with such nasty decisions, it is usually best to make them quickly, get into the new flow, and plan to course-correct going forward. This is a white-water rafting strategy, where hesitating on a split decision is the one behavior guaranteed to capsize the boat. When you do pick, go hard in the direction chosen, regardless of doubts. Just so with crossing the chasm.

The good news in this is that you do not have to pick the optimal beachhead to be successful. What you must do is win the beachhead you have picked. If there is a genuine problem in the segment, you will have the target customer pulling for you. If it is a hard problem, and the segment is reasonably small, you probably will not have competition to distract you. This means you can focus all your attention on the whole product, which is where it needs to be. Nail that and you win.

What could cause you to change course? Most often, it is that the scenario that is driving the effort is based on a false assumption. To guard against this, you should commission some market research early in the process specifically to validate the winning scenario. But you should not wait for this research to be complete before you start forward. The enemy in the chasm is always time. You must force the pace at all times, even when in doubt, because standing still plays into the hands of the established vendors and the status quo.

And Yes, Size Matters

Finally, when you are on the verge of making the commitment to the target segment, sooner or later the issue of how much revenue the segment might generate comes up. At this point, people normally think that bigger is better. But in fact, this is almost never the case. Here's why.

To become a going concern, a persistent entity in the market, you need a market segment that will commit to you as its de facto standard for enabling a critical business process. To become that de facto standard, you need to win at least half, and preferably a lot more, of the new orders in the segment over the next year. That is the sort of vendor performance that causes pragmatist customers to sit up and take notice. At the same time, you will still be taking orders from other segments. So do the math.

Suppose you can get half of next year's orders from the target segment—no mean feat considering that, prior to a couple of days ago, you hadn't focused on it at all. Say your revenue target is $10 million over all. That means $5 million from the target segment. It also means that same $5 million has to represent at least half of the total orders from the segment if you are to have the desired market-leader impact. In other words, if you are going to be a $10 million company next year you do not want to attack a segment larger than $10 million. At the same time, it should be large enough to generate your $5 million. So the rules of thumb in crossing the chasm are simple: *Big enough to matter, small enough to lead, good fit with your crown jewels.*

If you find the target segment is too big, sub-segment it. But be careful here. You must respect word-of-mouth boundaries. The goal is to become a big fish in a small pond, not one flopping about trying to straddle a couple of mud puddles. The best sub-segmentation is based on special interest groups within the general community. These typically are very tightly networked and normally form because they have very special problems to solve. In the absence of such, geography can often be a safe sub-segmentation variable, provided that it affects the way communities congregate.

If the target segment is too small to generate half of next year's sales for the new product, then you have to augment it. Again, be careful to respect genuine segmentation boundaries. If there is no appropriate super-segment, then you probably should go back and pick another target.

Recap: The Target Market Selection Process

We have been saying all along that the material in this chapter and the following three chapters is tactical by nature—that is, made up of relatively specific tasks and exercises that can, and should, be performed recurrently throughout a major enterprise. As a way of recapping this material, at the end of each chapter there will be a checklist of activities, suitable as a means either for managing a group through this process or testing the final output of a group's marketing decision making.

For selecting the target market segment that will serve as the point of entry for crossing the chasm into the mainstream market, the checklist is as follows:

1. Develop a library of target customer scenarios. Draw from

anyone in the company who would like to submit scenarios, but go out of your way to elicit input from people in customer-facing jobs. Keep adding to it until new additions are no more than minor variations on existing scenarios.

2. Appoint a subcommittee to make the target market selection. Keep it as small as possible but include on it anyone who could veto the outcome.

3. Number and publish the scenarios in typed form, one page per scenario. Accompanying the bundle, provide a spreadsheet with the rating factors assigned to columns and the scenarios assigned to rows. Break the rating factors into two subtotals, showstoppers first, then nice-to-haves.

4. Have each member of the subcommittee privately rate each scenario on the showstopper factors. Roll up individual ratings into a group rating. During this process discuss any major disagreements about scores. This typically surfaces different points of view on the same scenario and is critical not just to getting the opportunity correctly in focus but also in laying the groundwork for a future consensus that will stick.

5. Rank order the results and set aside scenarios that do not pass the first cut. This is typically about two-thirds of the submissions.

6. In a 400-degree oven, bake . . . (Oops! Wrong book. Sorry.) Repeat the private rating and public ranking process on the remaining scenarios with the remaining selection factors. Winnow the scenario population down to, at most, a favored few.

7. Depending on outcome, proceed as follows:

- *Group agrees on beachhead segment.* Go forward on that basis.
- *Group cannot decide among a final few.* Give the assignment to one person to build a bowling pin model of market development, incorporating as many of the final few as is reasonable, and calling out a head pin. Attack the head pin.
- *No scenario survived.* This does happen. In that case, do not attempt to cross the chasm. Also, do not try to grow. Continue to take early-market projects, keep burn rate as low as possible, and continue the search for a viable beachhead.

5

Assemble the Invasion Force

"I have always found you get a lot more in this world with a kind word and a gun than you do with just a kind word."

—Willie Sutton

Willie is only restating what any military leader will confirm: If you are committing an act of aggression, you'd better have the force to back it up. Or, to put this in terms closer to our immediate topic, marketing is *warfare—not wordfare.*

Which of us, about to launch an invasion, would prefer a good set of slogans to a good set of offensive and defensive weapons? Who would rather buy advertising time on television than missiles and munitions? Who would rather publish a manifesto than have guaranteed treaties with neighboring countries? Most high-tech executives—that's who.

There is a widespread perception among high-tech executives that marketing consists primarily of some long-range strategic thinking (when you can afford to take the time for it) and then a lot of tactical sales support—with nothing in between. In fact, marketing's most powerful contribution happens right in between. It is called *whole product marketing*, a term introduced earlier, and it is the fundamental basis for assembling the invasion force.

Consider the following scenario. When I was a salesman, I had a dream. The dream was simple. There was a monster bid coming up—with a $5 million minimum—and I had *wired* the request for proposal (RFP). I had, in the words of gamblers everywhere, a *mortal lock* on the thing. The client had met with me for long hours of consultation during which he had bought into every selling argument in favor of my product. He had then constructed the RFP so that only my product could get a 100 percent evaluation. The deal was mine. Then I woke up.

Okay—so that's a fantasy. But a version of that fantasy can be executed in the real world. We might call it *wiring the marketplace*. Again, the concept is simple. For a given target customer and a given application, create a marketplace in which your product is the only reasonable buying proposition. That starts, as we saw in the last chapter, with targeting markets that have a *compelling reason to buy* your product. The next step is to ensure that you have a monopoly over fulfilling that reason to buy.

To secure that monopoly, you need to understand 1) what a *whole product* consists of and 2) how to organize a marketplace to provide a whole product incorporating your company's offering.

The Whole Product Concept

One of the most useful marketing constructs in all of high-tech marketing is the concept of a whole product, an idea described in detail more than four decades ago in Theodore Levitt's *The Marketing Imagination*, and one that played a significant role a decade later in Bill Davidow's seminal *Marketing High Technology*. The concept is very straightforward: There is a gap between the marketing promise made to the customer—the compelling value proposition—and the ability of the shipped product to fulfill that promise. For that gap to be overcome, the product must be augmented by a variety of services and ancillary products to become the whole product.

The formal model, as diagrammed by Levitt, identifies four different levels of whole product completeness:

THE WHOLE PRODUCT MODEL

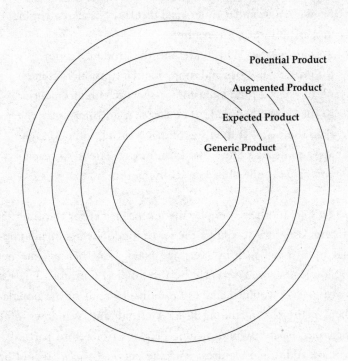

Potential Product

Augmented Product

Expected Product

Generic Product

1. *Generic product:* This is what is shipped in the box and what is covered by the purchasing contract.
2. *Expected product:* This is the product that the consumer thought she was buying when she bought the generic product. It is the *minimum* configuration of products and services necessary to have any chance of achieving the buying objective. For example, when you buy a tablet, you need to have either a Wi-Fi network at home or a cellular connection for it to work, but either one is likely to have to be purchased separately.
3. *Augmented product*: This is the product fleshed out to provide the *maximum* chance of achieving the buying objective. In the case of a tablet, this would include email, a browser, a calendar, a personal directory, a search engine, and an app store, for example.
4. *Potential product:* This represents the product's room for growth as more and more ancillary products come on the market and as customer-specific enhancements to the system are made. The fact that for the Apple iPad there are, at the time of this writing, some 374,090 apps on its App Store that I can buy to extend its reach and value is one of its key selling points.

To cite another example, the *generic product* for the Internet browser category would be the set of functions first made popular by Mosaic, then by Netscape Navigator, then by Internet Explorer, and most recently by Firefox and Chrome. The *expected product* would include portability to each of the popular client platforms, including IOS, Android, and Windows. The *augmented product* would include plug-ins from third parties to provide additional features. And the *potential product* would be the redefinition of the client, potentially to the exclusion of ever seeing the operating system—a world in which there are no device-specific apps, only HTML5 applets running ubiquitously. On the services side, for the generic product, there has to be at minimum an Internet service provider; for the expected product, a home page with a default search engine; for the augmented product, a variety of prearranged experiences presented as buttons or the like; and for the potential product, perhaps a complete reconstruction of consumer purchasing.

Now, at the introduction of any disruptive innovation, the marketing battle initially takes place at the level of the generic product—the thing in the center, the product itself. This is the hero in the battle for the *early market*. But as marketplaces develop, as we enter the *mainstream market*, products in the center become more and more alike, and the battle shifts increasingly to the outer circles. To understand how to dominate a mainstream marketplace we need to take a closer look at the significance of what Paul Harvey might once have called *the rest of the whole product*.

The Whole Product and the
Technology Adoption Life Cycle

First, let's look at how the whole product concept relates to crossing the chasm. If we look at the Technology Adoption Life Cycle as a whole, we can generalize that the outer circles of the whole product increase in importance as one moves from left to right. That is, the customers least in need of whole product support are the technology enthusiasts. They are perfectly used to cobbling together bits and pieces of systems and figuring out their own way to a whole product that pleases them. In fact, this is in large part the pleasure they take from technology products—puzzling through ways to integrate an interesting new capability into something they could actually use. Their motto: Real techies don't need whole products.

Visionaries, by contrast, take no pleasure in pulling together a whole product on their own, but they accept that, if they are going to be the first in their industry to implement the new system—and thereby gain a strategic advantage over their competitors—then they are going to have to take responsibility for creating the whole product under their own steam. The rise in interest in systems integration services is a direct response to increasing visionary interest in information systems as a source of strategic advantage. Systems integrators could just as easily be called whole product providers—that is their commitment to the customer.

So much for the market to the left of the chasm, the early market. To get to the right of the chasm—to cross into the mainstream market—you have to first meet the demands of the pragmatist customers. These customers want the whole product to be readily available from the outset. They like a product such as Microsoft Office because virtually every desktop and laptop supports it, files are exchangeable without fuss, there are books in every bookstore about how to use it, not to mention seminars for training, hotline support, and a whole cadre of temporary office workers already trained on its core products of Word, Excel, and PowerPoint. If instead the pragmatists are offered a "great deal" on an alternative suite of products—say, Google Apps, for example—they are reluctant to switch because they fear some part of the whole product will be missing, and they will be left holding the bag.

The same logic holds for why pragmatists prefer ARM's smartphone microprocessors to Intel's Atom, Google Search to Microsoft's Bing, Apple's iPhone to RIM's BlackBerry, HP printers to Epson's, Cisco routers to Huawei's. In every case, there is a risk that they are preferring an inferior product—if you look only at the generic product. But in every case, they are preferring the superior product if you look at the *whole* product.

To net this out: *Pragmatists evaluate and buy* whole *products*. The generic product, the product you ship, is a key part of the whole product, make no mistake. But once there are more than one or two comparable products in the marketplace, then investing in additional R&D at the generic level has a decreasing return, whereas there is an increasing return from marketing investments at the levels of the expected, the augmented, or the potential product. How to determine where to target these investments is the role of whole product planning.

Whole Product Planning

As we have just seen, the whole product model provides a key insight into the chasm phenomenon. The single most important difference between early markets and mainstream markets is that the former are willing to take responsibility for piecing together the whole product (in return for getting a jump on their competition), whereas the latter are not. Failure to recognize this principle has been the downfall of many a high-tech enterprise. Too often companies throw their products into the market as if they were tossing bales of hay off the back of a truck. There is no planning for the whole product—just the hope that their product will be so wonderful that customers will rise up in legions to demand that third parties rally about it. Well, God did divide the Red Sea for Moses.

For those who wish to take a more prudent course, however, whole product planning is the centerpiece for developing a market domination strategy. Pragmatists will hold off committing their support until they see a strong candidate for leadership emerge. Then they will back that candidate forcefully in an effort to squeeze out the other alternatives, thereby bringing about the necessary standardization to ensure good whole product development in their marketplace.

A good generic product is a great asset in this battle, but it is neither a necessary nor a sufficient cause of victory. Oracle did not have the best product when the market standardized on it. What Oracle offered instead was the best case for a viable whole product—a query language (SQL) based on an IBM standard plus all the major portability across hardware platforms plus an aggressive sales force to drive product into the market quickly. That is what the pragmatists in the IT department got behind.

In short, winning the whole product battle means winning the war. And because perception contributes to that reality, looking like you are winning the whole product battle is a key weapon to winning the war. On the other hand, *pretending* you are winning the whole product battle is a losing tactic—people check up on each other too much in the high-tech marketplace. These distinctions will become critically important in our next chapter, where we deal with *positioning*.

For now, our focus should be on the minimum commitment to whole product needed to cross the chasm. That is defined by the whole product that assures that the target customers can fulfill their compelling reason to buy. To work out how much whole product this is, you only need a simplified version of the whole model:

The Simplified Whole Product Model

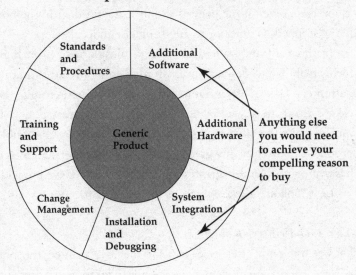

In the simplified model there are only two categories: 1) what we ship and 2) whatever else the customers need in order to achieve their compelling reason to buy. The latter is the *marketing promise* made to win the sale. The *contract* does not require the company to deliver on this promise, but the *customer relationship* does. Failure to meet this promise in a business-to-business market has extremely serious consequences. As the bulk of purchases in this marketplace are highly reference oriented, such failure can only create negative word of mouth, causing sales productivity to drop dramatically.

Classically, high tech has delivered 80 to 90 percent of a whole product to any number of possible target customers, but 100 percent to few, if any. Anything less than 100 percent, unfortunately, means that the customers either supply the remainder themselves or feel cheated. Significantly less than 100 percent means that the target market simply does not develop as forecast—even if the generic product, the product in the box being shipped, is superior to anything else in its class.

In short, if you wanted to trace disillusionment with high tech's inability to deliver on its promise to its investors and its customers, lack of attention to whole product marketing is the closest thing to a wellspring. This is actually great news—it means that the converse applies as well. By solving the whole product equation for any given set of target customers, high tech has overcome its single greatest obstacle to market development.

Let's look at an example to see how this works out.

The 3-D Printer, Revisited

Let's revisit our "after" scenario for the 3-D printer, the one where we are manufacturing designer lighting fixtures on demand. Here it is again:

New approach: David and his client have been reviewing catalogs and images over the Web for the better part of a week, and they have finally settled on a design. This is a variation on a couple of actual products that David has sketched out with input from the client. They take this design to a fixture wholesaler who supports 3-D printing. The wholesaler works with a freelance designer who is able to scan David's drawing and convert it into a CAD file. At the same time, the wholesaler works with David to select an appropriate material and finish for the fabricated fixture. Then both the CAD file and the material are fed into the printer, and out comes a finished fixture. If the client still wants to tweak it some more, this can be readily done by updating the file and printing it out

again. Further, by adjusting the parameters in the file, fixtures of different scales can be produced, all sharing the same
design.

Now, let's analyze this scenario in light of its implied whole
product commitments. There are several:

- *The wholesaler works with a freelance designer who is able to
  scan David's drawing and convert it into a CAD file.* The
  implication is that there is an industry-standard file
  format for such designs, perhaps one coming from Au-
  toCAD, sufficiently ubiquitous that its presence can be
  taken for granted.
- *The wholesaler works with David to select an appropriate material and finish for the fabricated fixture.* Here the assumption is that there preexists a fabrication material that can
  meet the demanding standards of David and his client.
  At the time of this writing, this is one of the weaker
  elements in the scenario.
- *If the client still wants to tweak it some more, this can be readily done by updating the file and printing it out again.* This
  assumes that the materials can be recycled or are cheap
  enough to discard. It also assumes that the printing can
  be done quickly enough that there is not a perennial
  backlog of print orders to get in the way.
- *By adjusting the parameters in the file, fixtures of different
  scales can be produced, all sharing the same design.* This
  assumes that the printer has few limitations on the size
  of the objects it can produce. Again, at the time of this
  writing, this is also a weak point in the scenario.

And so it goes. The point is, even a single target customer scenario implies a chain of commitments that any product manager serious about delivering a whole product to an emerging market opportunity must pursue to a satisfactory conclusion.

Now, in the case of a 3-D printer, one can readily imagine a fairly lengthy list of potential target customers and target applications. In addition to interior designers like David, one could imagine:

- *Industrial designers* prototyping parts for a piece of machinery. They would likely need a variety of durable materials in order to create and test the part under realistic conditions.
- *Toy manufacturers* creating custom toys. They would likely want vibrant primary colors to be part of the mix, not to mention assurances of zero toxicity.
- *Museum curators* making models of decaying artifacts. This would require a holographic scanner to create the 3-D file that the machine would replicate.
- *Footwear manufacturers* making shoes on demand. This would require material that was both fashionable and comfortable to wear, not to mention long lasting.
- *Antique car enthusiasts* making replacement parts that are no longer commercially available. Now we have to accept precision CAD files and extrude work in metal that can stand up to the stress of an operating engine.

As even this cursory listing indicates, *every additional new target customer will put additional new demands on the whole product.* That is, the total sum of products and services needed in order to get the desired benefit changes any time you change the value proposition. It soon becomes clear to even the most optimistic product marketing managers that they cannot go after all markets at once, that at minimum they have to sequence and prioritize opportunities, and that each opportunity has very real support costs.

Now, given the need for a whole product in order to fulfill the customer's reason to buy, what is the responsibility of the 3-D printer hardware vendor—and specifically of the product manager who has the 3-D printer as his responsibility—for seeing that this whole product is in fact delivered? The answer is, it has nothing to do with responsibility, it has to do with marketing success. If you leave your customer's success to chance, you are giving up control over your own destiny. Conversely, by thinking through your customer's problems—and solutions—in their entirety, you can define—and work to ensure that the customer gets—the whole product.

At no time is this marketing proposition more true than when crossing the chasm. Prior to the chasm there is some hope that the visionaries will backfill the whole product through their own systems integration efforts. Once the product is established in the mainstream, there is some hope that some third party will see an opportunity for itself to make money fleshing out the whole product. *But while you are crossing the chasm, there is no hope of any external support that is not specifically recruited by you for this purpose.*

Some Real-World Examples

To see how this works out in actual practice, let's turn now to some specific industry examples. Basically, there are two types of scenarios we want to work through—one where there is installed competition, and the other where there is not. In the former case, it is as if one were trying to invade Normandy from England, and the installed market leader were playing the role of the Nazi forces. In the latter, it is as if one had crossed the Pacific in 1492, landed on a new continent, and decided to set up shop selling wares to the natives. Neither task is for the faint of heart.

Aruba and Wireless Networks for Enterprises

To begin with the competitive example, imagine yourself back in 2006, leading a wireless networking company focused on bringing Wi-Fi to the enterprise. The name of the company is Aruba, which you may or may not have heard of. But you will have heard of the competitor they were targeting: *Cisco*!

Aruba at this point was growing very fast, but off a very small base, from $12 million in 2005 to $72 million in 2006—pretty amazing, to be sure, but enough to take on a competitor four hundred times its size? Welcome to the world of Silicon Valley start-ups. This is what you do. The only question to answer is, how?

The first rule is you have to leverage a point of disruption, one that puts the incumbent a bit back on its heels. In this case, wireless networks taken to their extreme threatened to cannibalize wireline networks, which were and still are the heart and soul of Cisco's franchise. Moreover, a new standard had just been released for Wi-Fi (802.11n, to be precise), which for the first time promised wireline performance delivered over the air. So there was a 10x value proposition potentially in play—arguably the single most pragmatic definition of a disruptive innovation.

The second rule is, remember the fish-to-pond ratio principle from the prior chapter, and target a market segment that is big enough to matter, small enough to lead, and a good fit with your crown jewels. Here small enough to lead means, in part, too small for the much bigger incumbent to spend a lot of time focusing on. Big fish have trouble competing in small niches.

For Aruba, applying this rule led them to the U.S. college and university market. At the time more and more students were coming to college with laptops. Arguably this was the first BYOD (bring-your-own-device) market segment, and as such it wanted networking services available everywhere, not just through a cable into a dorm room. Moreover, these students were not just doing searches and email anymore—they were also streaming music and video, which created an added push to adopt next-generation wireless standards early. And finally, colleges and universities like to support next-generation technology efforts from plucky start-ups, so they were more collaborative than a lot of other target markets would have been. All in all, targeting this market was a great call.

Now we come to the third rule, the one this chapter is about: Surround your disruptive core product, the thing that got you to the dance, with a whole product that solves for the target customer's problem end to end. That will keep you on the dance floor for a long time to come.

The way you design a whole product is to work backward from the target customer's use case, filling in the blanks as you go along, either with new R&D, an acquisition, a partnership, or an alliance. In the case of the college IT department deploying networking services across their campuses, the core product consisted of the following:

- A very large number of access points, as many as several thousand, to cover every point of access from the dorm to the library to the classroom to the student union, to sports facilities, and ultimately even to off-campus pubs (where a lot of professors keep their office hours).

- One or more mobility controllers, to manage all this traffic from a central point of control. This level of control had not been necessary in prior deployments where Wi-Fi networks were minor extensions to the wireline network, say covering guest services in a few conference rooms. But once the wireless network becomes the primary carrier of traffic, they are mandatory. For example, at the end of any exam, the entire class of students uploads their answers all at the same time, which can create a spike of demand—you don't want that to bring down your network, or to lose any test traffic, either.

- A network management system to support the network administrators, giving them the ability to dial service levels up or down, authenticate users, authorize access, as well as troubleshoot network outages and the like.

That covers the core product. What then would go into making up the whole product? Consider the following:

- The campuses still had wireline networks as well, even though they were not building them out as aggressively as they originally had planned. As a result, the network management system had to work both with the new and the old equipment. This led Aruba to partner with, and eventually acquire, AirWave, a network management system that grew up managing Cisco routers and switches.

- Additionally, most campuses had a student and faculty directory already in place, frequently Active Directory from Microsoft, so partnering here also became a priority.
- Then there were the students themselves, who were, well, let's say creative. As one network administrator said to Aruba, "Our security system is less focused on protecting our students from the world than it is on protecting the world from our students!" The era of Napster had come and gone by this point, but the era of BitTorrent file sharing, with or without authorization, was in full swing. Network administrators needed to shape this traffic at a minimum, if not shut it down upon demonstrable violations. This led Aruba to partner with and eventually to directly purchase from Bradford a network operations control center of the sort more often seen in telecommunications companies.
- In the continuing quest to compete for new students, colleges and universities had begun streaming content directly to digital devices, specifically video, both for education and for entertainment. This requires special video codecs to supply, which Aruba turned to a company called Video Furnace.
- As the market continued to develop, Aruba created an advisory board from its leading university customers, one member of which had the novel idea that, instead of using wireless to extend wireline, how about the other way around? Specifically, he asked for a remote access port that could be hooked into a wireline VPN (virtual private network) so that people at home or at other

remote locations could be part of the same network management system as well (no new log-ons, passwords, etc.). This Aruba had to invent, and it has subsequently become a key differentiator in its product line.

As you can see, nothing in the whole product is a showstopper from the point of a competitor seeking to neutralize Aruba's differentiation, but taken as a whole, for a large competitor who has much bigger fish to fry, it takes more focus to accomplish this outcome than it is worth. And from the customer's point of view, the fact that companies like Aruba are willing to go the extra mile just for them builds a level of loyalty that is long-lived indeed. This is the core dynamic that enables start-ups to cross the chasm despite direct opposition from installed incumbents.

Lithium and Customer-Enabled Tech Support

Now let's turn to the other scenario for crossing the chasm, the one where (good news) there is no enemy fortifying the shore against invasion because (bad news) people have yet to discover there is anything there to defend. Here the vendor must create a market out of whole cloth. Under these conditions, the pragmatist buyers who are the key to the mainstream market do not reject the new product so much as simply watch for signs of its adoption. They don't say no, in other words; they just don't say yes. Talk about extended sales cycles!

In this situation, entrepreneurs are fighting a race against time. Like the intrepid explorers and colonists of the sixteenth and seventeenth centuries, they have landed in terra incognita and have a fixed amount of supplies (working capital) to see them through to self-sufficiency. The question is not whether someday someone will make a successful colony; the question is whether it will be them, or whether they will die in the attempt. Have we landed at Plymouth Rock or Jamestown?

Let's look at a specific example. Lithium is a SaaS (software-as-a-service) company that creates online communities of consumers and customers, to co-create and share digitally delivered marketing, sales, and customer support content. When they were founded just after the dot-com bust at the beginning of the century, this was a novel idea, and Lithium's claim to fame was that its founders were online game developers who had learned a ton about how to motivate voluntary behavior through virtual rewards. The idea caught on with early adopters, but as you might expect, the pragmatists adopted a wait-and-see attitude. To cross the chasm, Lithium had to target a pragmatist enclave disaffected with the status quo. They found that enclave in tech support.

Tech support organizations are, as a rule, overworked and underappreciated. The problem is that most tech products interoperate with so many other tech products, it is a real challenge to figure out what or who is at fault when something goes wrong. The people who might know these answers get paid way too much to staff a customer support hotline, and the people on the hotline—who often as not are in a call center somewhere across the Pacific Ocean—have to work with scripts as best they can. Anyone who has been on one of these calls can testify how frustrating a customer experience it can be.

So what if we could end all that? What if you could go online and get expert advice from the very best minds in the industry, and better still, get it all for free? Wouldn't that be cool? Dell thinks so. So does HP, and Lenovo, and Autodesk, and Microsoft. Welcome to the world of customer-enabled tech support.

The key idea here is to create an online community where customers can answer other customers' questions before they even get to a customer support hotline. Why would people with such expertise spend their time doing this? Technology enthusiasts (remember them from the very beginning of the Technology Adoption Life Cycle model?) like to help other people. It is their passion. If you add some game-oriented rewards and social recognition (what people now call *gamification*, although that word still grates on an ex-English-professor's ears), it works even better.

The core product here is a branded website that lets customers both ask and answer questions, lets them rate the quality of the answers, which over time allows the best answerers to emerge, garnering these providers the highest status awards. That is the core product, and it is highly disruptive wherever the status quo consists of out-of-date knowledge bases being consulted by inexpert call center employees, backed up by harried engineers who have neither time nor patience to answer the same questions over and over again.

But the truth is, creating a wiki-like site to perform these kinds of functions is not that hard. So what could Lithium do to build a whole product that would win over the skeptical pragmatists? To be fair, they did have one thing going for them right out of the chute. The cost reduction of deflecting a call from a call center to a website is substantial—as much as ten times. And since call centers are cost centers in most tech enterprises, reducing costs is always top of mind. But here's what Lithium did over and above that allowed them to cross the chasm and win the market leading position in this niche. (Full disclosure: In case I sound a bit enthusiastic here, I should reveal that I joined the company's board of directors in 2012.)

- Helped customers create their *tribal knowledge bases*.
  Lithium provided consulting support to help customers

curate the ever-growing body of user-contributed content, turning community conversations into knowledge articles, making this content easier to find and easier to consume. This approach to crowd-sourcing increases customer satisfaction, reduces mean time to getting the right answer, increases call deflection, and increases customer loyalty, especially among the committed few who contribute much of the most valuable content.

- Extended the support to *mobile devices*. Most Web content is challenging to consume on a mobile device, but increasingly that is what the consumer or customer has ready to hand when they need an answer. This not only makes life more convenient for the end user; it dramatically increases call deflection because the consumer can switch from one to the other while using the same device.

- Integrated their service with the enterprise's CRM (Customer Relationship Management) system. This connects the customers using Lithium with enterprise employees, allowing the latter to address unanswered questions, capture feedback and insights to feed back to developers, and further improve the knowledge base that drives the overall system.

- Extended support to the social web (Facebook, Twitter, Google+, etc.). This is part of an "omni-channel" movement throughout tech to engage the consumer and customer on the device and in the environment that best suits them. It allows for the knowledge base and the community population to extend themselves seamlessly by adding links to other sites and individuals.

By extending their core product to create a whole product, Lithium was meeting the needs both of their immediate target customers—consumer tech companies—and their customers' customers, the consumers themselves needing help and the technology enthusiasts looking to share their expertise.

Partners and Allies

"Strategic alliances" with partners and allies have always been trendy items in high-tech marketing. One expects to see ads on Facebook reading:

> Large, well-heeled company with established distribution channels and aging product line seeks small, entrepreneurial, cash-starved technology leader with hot new product. Photos available upon request. . . .

As a rule, however, these types of alliances do better in PowerPoint presentations than on the street. To start with, the company cultures are normally too antithetical to cooperate with each other. Decision cycles are wildly out of sync, leading to enormous frustration among the entrepreneurs and patronizing responses from the established management. To make matters worse, each side has probably misrepresented itself one way or another during partnership negotiations, such that there is plenty of ammunition for each group to fire at the other once tempers get hot. This is particularly likely to be the case when the entrepreneurs have been angling for acquisition as an exit strategy. So, for the most part, despite the impeccable logic of these mergers, they are very tough to bring off.

Of course, some strategic alliances have been extremely successful. Consider the relationship that developed among SAP, Hewlett-Packard, and Andersen Consulting to displace IBM as the premier enterprise vendor by bringing client-server Enterprise Resource Planning (ERP) systems to market. Or consider the alliance between Intel and Microsoft, what some have called the Wintel duopoly, which to this day orchestrates the PC industry. And more recently, Cisco, EMC, and VMware have teamed up to create a Unified Computing Environment for cloud computing that is having substantial success.

All these alliances have been hugely powerful and moved mountains of market cap. Note, however, that they are among relatively equally matched peers. And even with that proviso, the complexities of developing and maintaining such strategic alliances in the field, where sales actually happen, are sufficient to make even the most experienced organizations struggle. They are certainly not the province of mere product managers seeking to ensure that their niche-segment target customers achieve their compelling reasons to buy.

What does work for product managers, on the other hand, are tactical "whole product" alliances. These alliances have one and only one purpose: *Accelerate the formation of whole product infrastructure within a specific target market segment in support of a segment-specific compelling reason to buy.* The basic commitment is to codeliver a whole product and market it cooperatively. This benefits the whole product manager by ensuring customer satisfaction. It also benefits the whole product partners by expanding their marketplace without them having to do any of the marketing. As long as each side lives up to its part of the bargain, there is good reason to expect success.

Whole product alliances are readily initiated and managed

at the product marketing manager level. Typically, the initial opportunity is first brought to the company's attention either by the salespeople or by customer support staff, one of whom has bumped into the potential ally at a particular customer's site. But they can also be anticipated through the exercise of thinking through the whole product solution to the customer's buying objective. The main point, again, is that these are tactical alliances growing out of whole product needs, not strategic alliances growing out of . . . well, whatever strategic alliances grow out of (my personal feeling is that the number-one cause of strategic alliances is too many staff people with not enough to do).

Partners and Allies: The Example of Rocket Fuel

To see how this might work out in a few specific instances, let's first consider the example of Rocket Fuel, a Mohr Davidow investment that has achieved meteoric growth in the digital advertising sector. Like most things in the new digital economy, it "takes a village" to create, launch, monitor, and monetize a digital ad campaign. Rocket Fuel's role in this ecosystem is to increase the yield of digital advertising by placing the right ad in front of the right person at the right time—all done by artificial intelligence algorithms made increasingly effective through machine learning. Needless to say, this is a highly specialized capability.

Specialized offerings must focus intensely on what is *core* to their differentiation, which means that spending anything on context dilutes their ability to scale their value and size. As a result, companies taking this path must look to leverage existing systems and players wherever they can. This requires a whole host of "silent" partners and allies, totally necessary to the whole product, economically aligned with, in this case, Rocket Fuel's value proposition, but not able or willing to actively engage in a lot of partnering activities.

The key tactic here is to build very clean interfaces for accessing other systems and letting them access you—whether they be computer systems like *digital ad exchanges*, where publishers can put their inventory and advertisers can bid on it in real time, or whether they be industry participants like *ad agencies* and *media buyers*, who have big budgets they need to put to work effectively and efficiently. In the case of Rocket Fuel their goal is to look like "any other" *media partner*, just one that delivers much more bang for the same buck.

In addition to the principals directly involved, there are peripheral partnering relationships that can grease the skids to accelerate adoption in your target market. In the case of Rocket Fuel the Interactive Advertising Board played a key role in standardizing contracts such that a small company could play across a broad footprint without having to have a legal department the size of Chicago. And the reporting capabilities of the *ad servers*, like DART and Atlas, helped make transparent the performance metrics upon which Rocket Fuel was basing its entire value proposition—no more "I know I waste half of my ad budget, but I just don't know which half." Now Rocket Fuel's customers did, with no investment required from the company itself.

The net of all this is that the advertising industry as a whole, realizing that consumer attention has migrated online in a big way, has collectively rallied around companies like Rocket Fuel and AudienceScience and Visible Measures (to name three of MDV's investments in the area) because everyone in the ecosystem has a vested interest in engaging consumers across this new medium. The lesson for everyone else is clear: If you want to go fast, go alone; if you want to go far, go with others. In the age of the Internet you need to do both at the same time, and that's where whole product partners can make all the difference.

That said, Rocket Fuel is something of a special case—not all fast-growing businesses in digital commerce depend so intensely on big data and analytics. Some actually depend primarily on people! Take Infusionsoft, for example.

Partners and Allies: The Example of Infusionsoft

Infusionsoft is another MDV-invested software-as-a-service company, one that provides sales and marketing services (what the tech industry calls CRM—Customer Relationship Management) to small businesses (typically fewer than twenty-five employees, many no more than one or two). It was founded to help truly small business owners make the transition to online marketing, a capability that can be transformative if used properly, but highly daunting to adopt, especially for those new to either digital or marketing or both.

This created an initial conundrum for Infusionsoft—how do you attract typically late-adopting target customers to a technology they are not themselves engaging with? Online marketing only works, after all, if your target customer is online. The company solved this problem by partnering with a cadre of *small business marketing experts* who made their living selling seminars to small business owners advocating the new online approach. These gurus were able to attract prospects in droves, and what better way to stay in touch with them than to help them install an online marketing capability? The software reinforced the teachings, and the teachings reinforced the software. To be sure, this was still a congregation of early adopters, but it helped Infusionsoft meet its first growth milestones.

To cross the chasm, however, the company needed to expand beyond the early market for marketing innovation and access the pragmatist majority. It experimented with a number of possible beachhead markets, and had particular success with professional speakers (a more generalized version of the marketing guru segment), fitness studios, and dentists (these last two both having a "retention marketing" objective that particularly lent itself to online reminders).

In conjunction with these forays it also tried an experiment that failed. Instead of charging customers what had been a hefty up-front fee to get them up and running, it waived the fee entirely, thereby vastly increasing the number of prospects willing to sign up. Unfortunately, a large number of those same customers churned out after a short period. Painful as that was, it taught an important lesson about the whole product: Onboarding, both for technical and for business process reengineering reasons, had to be carefully supervised.

By adding back a lower-cost version of their onboarding service, Infusionsoft was able to drive down its churn and achieve its targeted retention rate goals. But this raised a second challenge: How could you scale the company to meet the escalating demand without creating a low-margin call center environment? This challenge was made even more acute when the company expanded from a pure marketing service to an end-to-end CRM offer.

The good news here is that nature abhors a vacuum. The fact that Infusionsoft customers were willing to pay several thousand dollars to be guided through their onboarding and coached through their first several marketing campaigns was not lost on the service providers in their ecosystem. A number of them began to throw their hats in the ring to provide the same service.

This led the company to host an Implementation Accelerator workshop, in which they brought twenty-five customers together with a complete suite of experts for a two-day "marketing hackathon." Included in the effort were Infusionsoft *success coaches* to help with inventing marketing strategy and tactics, *copywriters*, *script writers* and *videographers*, *software object designers*, and *webmasters*, not to mention Infusionsoft's own tech support staff. What some customers were able to accomplish in two days exceeded what many had done in an entire year. Clearly smoothing the pathway to a whole product was a critical success factor.

This led the company to create a training and certification program that in the past two years has graduated more than two hundred *Infusionsoft Certified Consultants*, not one of whom is on the company's payroll. Moreover, because each hand washes the other, these same consultants are a strong source of referrals, driving more than half of the company's new customer enrollments in the most recent fiscal year.

The lesson here is clear: While strategic partnerships often struggle mightily to sustain their engagement and maintain their relevance, whole product partnerships built around whole products for specific target markets with compelling reasons to buy do not. That said, let's see how these same principles can be applied in a strategic partnering scenario.

Partners and Allies: The Example of Mozilla

While I clearly favor the tactical path, there are cases in high tech when you simply have to take a top-down, orchestrate-the-industry approach. Such was the challenge facing the team at Mozilla in 2011 when they made the commitment to expand their world-renowned Firefox browser franchise from the desktop to the mobile device.

Firefox is an open-source Web browser that came into existence largely to remediate the flaws in Microsoft's Internet Explorer 7.0. That particular piece of technology put the end user's computer at the mercy of spammers in unacceptable ways, and the team at Mozilla led an effort to create a "people's choice" alternative. It worked, with 100 million downloads in the first year, leading it to becoming the third most popular browser in the world behind Internet Explorer and Google Chrome. It also worked in another way, spurring both Microsoft and Google to adopt "Do Not Track" optionality into their latest releases, thereby helping to fulfill Mozilla's populist mission.

Mission accomplished? Well, not so fast. How about the next two billion people who are expected to come on to the Internet in the next few years for the first time, people from developing economies who have never had Web access before? They will be using mobile devices for sure—what browser will be their standard?

To continue its mission of populist values, Mozilla needed to orchestrate the mobile industry to create a mobile browser that could perform at a smartphone level, competing directly with Apple and Google Android devices, and to organize the entire ecosystem to support this open-source platform as a de facto standard. Mobile is an amazingly diverse sector, ranging from very conservative national telephony franchises to over-the-top technology disrupters coming from all sides. How could a small not-for-profit company in Mountain View, California, hope to paint anything coherent on such a large canvas?

Here's what they did do:

1. Targeted the "next two billion" Web users, embracing the constraint that they would not be able to afford anything more than free open-source software, but who would be willing to accept a product optimized for price/performance as opposed to the latest features, and who would require a hyper-low-cost platform, which they had the technology to deliver.

2. Recruited two key *mobile operators*—Telefonica and Deutsche Telekom—to anchor this effort because, as their CEO at the time, Gary Kovacs, put it, "They write the checks."

3. Leveraged their support to recruit two key *device manufacturers*—ZTE and TCL (formerly Alcatel) to supply Firefox-enabled devices.

4. Held summits, councils, and multi-party planning days over the course of more than a year to get the ecosystem aligned both at the executive and the operating levels.

5. Fought to maintain a common core set of standards for the platform, despite pressure from every side to support "specials," so that the end result was truly scalable at a global level.

6. Led a launch at the 2013 Mobile World Congress where Kovacs was joined onstage by twenty-three other CEOs, each of whom had signed a commitment to launch a Firefox-enabled device in at least one country.

Not bad for an organization whose mission in life is to champion individual rights in an age of superpowers.

A key takeaway here is that the steps of market development outlined in this book structured their entire effort:

- They began with a target customer (disenfranchised citizens in developing economies who would be making their very first purchase of an Internet-enabled service) with a compelling reason to buy (access to all the content on the Web for free, plus communications for personal, family, and business purposes).
- They figured out the whole product and determined for that product that the operators and the OEM device manufacturers were the critical anchor partners.
- They then went after partners who shared their interest in the next two billion, with franchise interests in developing economies, and used their focused requests to create a big enough sales opportunity to get the attention of two world-class OEMs.
- When it came time to "create the competition" (something we will get to in the next chapter), the whole ecosystem knew it was Apple and Google, two extremely powerful ecosystems who in flexing their muscles were making both operators and OEMs increasingly nervous such that they were ready to support the entry of a balancing force.

Finally, at no point did they try to make the story or the value proposition about themselves. It was always an effort in service to the world and to the industry, so people could buy in based on their own self-interest, not just in order to get a "good deal." That is a true key to whole product management success.

The net result of the partnering activities we have been reviewing in the cases of Rocket Fuel, Infusionsoft, and Mozilla is the *creation of a market*. For markets represent more than just a buyer and a seller. They are an ecology of interrelated interests interoperating to create what business schools call value chains. For any company crossing the chasm, fostering the initial partnerships to create the whole product is the equivalent of seeding the value chain, getting it started. Once value starts being generated, a free-market system becomes self-reinforcing, and the whole product manager's job then is simply to let go and get out of the way.

To sum up, whole product definition followed by a strong program of tactical alliances to speed the development of the whole product infrastructure is the essence of assembling an invasion force for crossing the chasm. The force itself is a function of actually delivering on the customer's compelling reason to buy in its entirety. That force is still rare in the high-tech marketplace, so rare that, despite the overall high-risk nature of the chasm period, *any company that executes a whole product strategy competently has a high probability of mainstream market success.*

Recap: Tips on Whole Product Management

1. Use the doughnut diagram to define—and then to communicate—the whole product. Shade in all the areas for which you intend your company to take primary responsibility. The remaining areas must be filled either by the customer or by partners or allies.

2. Review the whole product to ensure it has been reduced to its minimal set. This is the KISS philosophy (Keep It Simple, Stupid). It is hard enough to manage a whole product without burdening it with unnecessary bells and whistles.

3. Review the whole product from each participant's point of view. Make sure each vendor wins, and that no vendor gets an unfair share of the pie. Inequities here, particularly when they favor you, will instantly defeat the whole product effort—companies are naturally suspicious of each other anyway, and given any encouragement, will interpret your entire scheme as a rip-off.

4. Develop the whole product relationships slowly, working from existing instances of cooperation toward a more formalized program. Do not try to institutionalize cooperation in advance of credible examples that everyone can benefit from it—not the least of whom should be the customers. Also, do not recruit directly competing partners to serve the same need in the same segment—this will only discourage them from making a full commitment to your program.

5. With large partners, try to work from the bottom up; with small ones, from the top down. The goal in either case is to work as close as possible to where decisions that affect the customer actually get made.

6. Once formalized relationships are in place, use them as openings for communication only. Do not count on them to drive cooperation. Partnerships ultimately work only when specific individuals from the different companies involved choose to trust each other.

7. If you are working with very large partners, focus your energy on establishing relationships at the district sales office level and watch out for wasting time and effort with large corporate staffs. Conversely, if you are working with small partners, be sensitive to their limited resources and

do everything you can to leverage your company to work to their advantage.

8. Finally, do not be surprised to discover that the most difficult partner to manage is your own company. If the partnership really is equitable, you can count on someone inside your company insisting on taking a bigger share of the benefit pie. In fighting back, look to your customers to be your truest and most powerful allies.

6

Define the Battle

On the eve of our invasion, let us regroup. We have already established the point of attack, a target market segment plagued by a problem that gives it a truly compelling reason to buy. We have already mapped out the whole product needed to eliminate this problem and have recruited the necessary partners and allies to deliver it. The major obstacle now is competition. To succeed in securing our beachhead we need to understand who or what the competition is, what their current relationship to our target customer consists of, and how we can best position ourselves to drive them out of our target market segment.

This is what we mean by defining the battle. *The fundamental rule of engagement is that any force can defeat any other force—if it can define the battle.* If we get to set the turf, if we get to set the competitive criteria for winning, why would we ever lose? The answer, depressingly enough, is because we don't do it right. Sometimes it is because we misunderstand either our own strengths and weaknesses, or those of our competitors. More often, however, it is because we misinterpret what our target customers really want, or we are afraid to step up to the responsibility of making sure they get it.

How far must one go to serve one's customers? Well, in the

case of crossing the chasm, one of the key things a pragmatist customer insists on seeing is viable competition. If you are fresh from
developing a new value proposition with visionaries, that competition is not likely to exist—at least not in a form that a pragmatist
would appreciate. What you have to do then is create it.

Creating the Competition

In the progression of the Technology Adoption Life Cycle, the
nature of competition changes dramatically. These changes are
so radical that, in a very real sense, one can say at more than one
point in the cycle that one has no obvious competition. Unfortunately, where there is no competition, there is no market. By
way of introduction, therefore, we need to rethink the significance of competition as it relates to crossing the chasm.

In our experience to date with developing an early market,
competition has not come from competitive products so much
as from alternative modes of operation. Resistance has been a
function of inertia growing out of commitment to the status quo,
fear of risk, or lack of a compelling reason to buy. Our goal in the
early market has been to enlist visionary sponsors to help overcome this resistance. Their competition, in turn, has come from
others within their own company, pragmatists who are vying
with visionaries for dollars to fund projects. The pragmatists'
competitive solution, in general, is to invest dollars to chip away
at problems a piece at a time (whereas the visionaries aspire, like
Alexander the Great with the Gordian knot, to cut through them
with a single mighty—and mighty expensive—stroke). Pragmatists work to educate the company on the risks and costs involved.
Visionaries counter with charismatic appeals to taking bold and

decisive actions. The competition takes place at the level of corporate agenda, not at the level of competing products.

That's how competitions work in the early market. It is not at all how they work in the mainstream, in part because there are not enough visionaries to go around, and in part because visionaries themselves like to play not in the mainstream but rather out in front of it. Now we are in the true domain of the pragmatist. *In the pragmatist's domain, competition is defined by comparative evaluations of products and vendors within a common category.*

These comparative evaluations confer on the buying process an air of rationality that is extremely reassuring to the pragmatist, the sort of thing that manifests itself in evaluation matrices of factors weighted and scored. And the conclusions drawn from these matrices will ultimately shape the dimensions and segmentation of the mainstream market. Traditional desktop PCs, where Windows still has the edge, are still thought best for office automation, while laptops, where Apple has made a big incursion, are better for working on the go, tablets (an even stronger Apple position) for leveraging computing in meetings, and smartphones, where Google Android holds the high ground, for being online 24/7, all of which has led to an increasing preference for wireless over wireline networks, putting Cisco on notice. All this is music to the ears of pragmatist buyers who do not like to buy until there is both established competition and an established leader, for that is a signal that the market has matured sufficiently to support a reasonable whole product infrastructure around an identified centerpiece.

In sum, the pragmatists are loath to buy until they can compare. *Competition, therefore, becomes a fundamental condition for purchase.* So, coming from the early market, where there are typically no perceived competing products, with the goal of penetrating the mainstream, you often have to go out and *create your competition.*

Creating the competition is the single most important marketing communication decision made in the battle to enter the mainstream. It begins with positioning your product within a buying category that already has some established credibility with the pragmatist buyers. That category should be populated with other reasonable buying choices, ideally ones with which the pragmatists are already familiar. Within this universe, your goal is to position your product as the indisputably correct buying choice.

The great risk here is to rig the competition, that is, to create a universe that is too self-serving. You can succeed in creating a competitive set that you clearly dominate, but this set, unfortunately, is either not credible or not attractive to the pragmatist buyers. For example, I might claim that I am the greatest high-tech marketing consultant with a Ph.D. in Renaissance English literature. This claim might be credible, but it is not particularly attractive. On the other hand, I might claim that I am the greatest marketing consultant of all time—an attractive claim, perhaps (although it is not obvious to me how one can be a great consultant and egotistical at the same time), but, in any event, not a credible one.

So, how can you avoid selecting a self-serving or irrelevant competitive set? The key is to focus in on the values and concerns of the pragmatists, not the visionaries. It helps to start with the right conceptual model—in this case, *the Competitive Positioning Compass*. That model is designed to create a value profile of target customers anywhere in the Technology Adoption Life Cycle, identify what to them would appear to be the most reasonable competitive set, develop comparative rankings within that set on the value attributes with the highest ranking in their profile, and then build our positioning strategy development around those comparative rankings. Here's how it works:

The Competitive Positioning Compass

There are four domains of value in high-tech marketing: technology, product, market, and company. As products move through the Technology Adoption Life Cycle, the domain of greatest value to the customer changes. In the early market, where decisions are dominated by technology enthusiasts and visionaries, the key value domains are technology and product. In the mainstream, where decisions are dominated by pragmatists and conservatives, the key domains are market and company. Crossing the chasm, in this context, represents a transition from product-based to market-based values.

The Competitive-Positioning Compass illustrates these dynamics:

THE COMPETITIVE-POSITIONING COMPASS

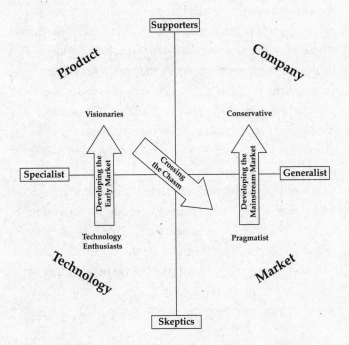

There is a lot of information packed into this model, so let's sort it out piece by piece:

- The directionality provided by the compass comes in the form of the two labeled axes. The horizontal dimension shows the range of buyer interest in and understanding of high-technology issues. In general, the early market is dominated by specialists who, by their nature, are more interested in technology and product issues than in market standing or company stature. By contrast, the mainstream is dominated by generalists who are more interested in market leadership and company stability than in the bits and bytes or speeds and feeds of particular products.

- The vertical dimension overlays a second measure, the buyer's attitude toward the proposed value proposition, ranging from skepticism to support. Markets begin in a state of skepticism and evolve to a state of support. In the case of the early market, the technology enthusiasts are the skeptical gatekeepers; in the case of the mainstream market, it is the pragmatists. Once they have given their blessings, then their companions—visionaries and conservatives, respectively—feel free to buy in.

- The model also points to the fact that people who are supportive of your value proposition take an interest in your products and in your company. *People who are skeptical of you do not.* This means that, at the beginning of a market, when skepticism is the common state, basing communications on product or company strengths is a mistake. You have no permission to tout these elements because the market players do not yet believe you are going to be around long enough to make a difference.

- However, there are ways to win over skeptics. Even the most skeptical specialists are always on the lookout for new technology breakthroughs. Thus, although you cannot initially get them to sponsor your product, you can get them involved in understanding its technology, and from that understanding, to gain an appreciation for the product itself. The more they appreciate the technology, the easier it becomes for them to support the product.

- Similarly, skeptical generalists may not take an interest in an unproven company but are always interested in new market developments. If you can show the generalists that there is an emerging unmet market requirement, one that you have specifically positioned your products and your marketing efforts to meet, then out of their appreciation for the market opportunity, they can learn to appreciate your company.

- These are the two "natural" marketing rhythms in high tech—developing the early market and developing the mainstream market. You develop an early market by demonstrating a strong technology advantage and converting it to product credibility, and you develop a mainstream market by demonstrating a market leadership advantage and converting it to company credibility.

- By contrast, the "chasm transition" represents an unnatural rhythm. Crossing the chasm requires moving from an environment of support among the visionaries back into one of skepticism among the pragmatists. It means moving from the familiar ground of

product-oriented issues to the unfamiliar ground of
market-oriented ones, and from the familiar audience
of like-minded specialists to the unfamiliar audience of
wary generalists.

Now let's tie all this back into creating the competition. If we
are going to succeed in winning over the lower right quadrant, the
skeptical pragmatists, then any dialogue about an emerging competitive set has to be based in market-oriented concerns. That's
what the pragmatists care about. In other words, we must shift our
marketing focus from celebrating product-centric value attributes
to market-centric ones. Here is a representative list of each:

PRODUCT-CENTRIC	MARKET-CENTRIC
<u>Cool product</u>	<u>Most complete whole product</u>
Easy to use	Solid user experience
Elegant architecture	Compatibility with standards
Product price	Whole product price
Unique functionality	Situational value
	Fit for purpose

In the previous chapter, the entire basis of the focus on
whole product and partners and allies was to move our leadership premise from the left-hand list to the right. That is, lacking
an existing market leadership position, we wanted, within the
confines of a manageable market segment, to create the valued
attributes of one, and thereby bring a state of true market leadership into existence. Now we need to communicate what we
have accomplished so as to win the pragmatist buyers' support.

To sum up, it is the market-centric value system—supplemented (but not superseded) by the product-centric one—that must be the basis for the value profile of the target customers when crossing the chasm.

This value profile, in turn, will model how the target customers are likely to perceive the competitive set and what position they are likely to accord to a new player coming into that set.

More specifically, creating the competition involves using two competitors as beacons so that the market can locate your company's unique value proposition. The first of these two competitors we will call the *market alternative*. This is a vendor that the target customer has been buying from for years. The problem they address is the one we will address, and the budget that is allocated to them represents the money we as the new entrant are going to preempt. To earn the right to this budget, we are going to use a disruptive innovation to address a stubbornly problematic limitation in the traditional offer.

The second reference competitor we will call the *product alternative*. This is a company that is also harnessing the same disruptive innovation we are—or at least close to it—and is positioning itself like us as a technology leader. Their very existence gives credibility to the notion that now is the time to embrace this new discontinuity. Our intent here is to acknowledge their technology but to differentiate from them by virtue of our own segment-specific focus.

Let's see how this plays out in a couple of concrete examples.

Creating the Competition: The Example of Box

With the advent of consumer computing at the turn of the twenty-first century, a host of new offerings raced to take advantage of the proliferation of cloud computing services. One of the most successful was Dropbox, a very simple file-sharing utility that let consumers exchange photos, music, and the like. It was so easy to use that workgroups in enterprises began to leverage it as well. Not surprisingly, however, given its focus on consumer ease of use, Dropbox did not invest as heavily in enterprise features as IT departments demand, and so the search went out for a more enterprise-oriented alternative. Enter Box.

The challenge Box faced was that enterprises already had a widely proliferated solution for end-user file sharing called SharePoint from Microsoft. At the same time Dropbox was a better-known brand with an established consumer appeal. How could Box win here?

Actually, it turns out this is the perfect positioning situation. SharePoint represented the viable *market alternative* while Dropbox represented the viable *product alternative*. All Box had to do was position itself at the intersection—Dropbox's ease of use meets SharePoint's enterprise standards. Best of both worlds.

This intersection is easily captured in a simple 2x2 matrix, as follows:

	OLD TECH	NEW TECH
Target Market	Market Alternative	**YOU**
Broader Market		Product Alternative

The two alternatives called out in this diagram are your *reference competitors*. In the case of Box, by calling out Microsoft as its market alternative, it makes clear that it is going after the same use cases and the same budget inside the enterprise. At the same time, by calling out Dropbox as its product alternative, it makes clear that its disruptive innovation is radical ease of use. The company still has to deliver on these promises and still has to compete vigorously to win, but nobody is confused about what game it is playing.

Creating the Competition: The Example of WorkDay

Back in the 1990s, at the beginning of the client-server software era in which PCs replaced terminals as end-user access devices, the first great success in packaged enterprise applications was PeopleSoft. It crossed the chasm targeting the HR department, providing a whole suite of interactive functions that had never been made available before.

As the decade unfolded, however, and the market shifted from a "best of breed" orientation to a preference for integrated suites, PeopleSoft lost ground to two much larger rivals, Oracle and SAP. Then in the tech downturn of 2002, Oracle initiated a hostile and highly contested takeover that led ultimately to its acquisition of the firm.

The founders of PeopleSoft, however, were not done yet. They could see that another shift was under way in enterprise software, perhaps even more profound than the transition to client-server: software-as-a-service applications running on top of cloud computing. It was still early days, but they set out once again to disrupt the HR marketplace.

What did they have to do to communicate their new position? Well, the market already knew them as the founders of PeopleSoft, so they just used that very product as their market alternative. And for their product alternative, they picked the hottest SaaS company on the planet, Marc Benioff's Salesforce.com.

Again, the message was unmistakable. We are going after the installed base of PeopleSoft customers, the people "we" sold and that Oracle now "owns." And we are bringing to them all the benefits of software-as-a-service—pay as you go, continuous releases, low switching costs—the very things that the old client server paradigm simply cannot match.

Just to be perfectly clear here, as I noted before with Box, WorkDay still has an uphill battle taking on an entrenched incumbent like Oracle. But by thoughtful use of reference competitors, what they do not have to struggle with is explaining their value proposition.

Let's close this section by looking at two companies that have not been so fortunate.

Failing to Create the Competition: The Examples of Segway and Better Place

Segway at its launch was something of the Google Glass of its era—an extraordinary technology that looked, well, pretty dorky. In case you have never seen one, a Segway looks like an upright lawn mower that you stand on, and simply by leaning in the direction you want to go, it motors you there. This is all made possible by truly superior gyroscopic technology that keeps you balanced, or rather just off balance, to move you along.

The company was backed by Kleiner Perkins, at the time arguably the leading venture capital firm in the world, and was launched with great fanfare as the new people mover. Anybody who walked for a living was going to now ride—mail carriers, cops on the beat, meter readers, door-to-door salespeople, you name it. And then, well, they ran into the problem of stairs. And that definitely restricted the field of application.

Still, there are plenty of flat places around, and more every day with all the investment in access, so why hasn't the product been able to make any headway? One explanation is that it was unable to find a pair of reference competitors that made its position make sense. There really is no market alternative out there. That is to say, there is no people mover budget to target. The closest you could get would be motorbikes or motorized wheelchairs or maybe golf carts, but none of these was close enough. And on the product side, there were no other companies leveraging this kind of disruptive technology in other market segments, so again, no way to cross-reference to success elsewhere.

Segway was all by itself, and that is not a good place to be when you are trying to cross the chasm. The same held true for what looked like a much more reasonable proposition in the electric vehicle space, Shai Agassi's Better Place.

Better Place was founded on a terrific value proposition. Electric vehicles were clearly the coming thing, but charging them took so long, you could only drive them under restricted use cases. But what if the battery packs were swappable? Then you could go into a recharging station, drop off the old pack, insert a new one, and be on your way. Of course, you might risk getting stuck with a dud pack, so the way to solve for that was to have the infrastructure run, end to end, as a public utility, with the consumer simply "buying miles" the way a cell phone customer buys minutes.

The idea was compelling enough to raise $850 million. But it never could get off the ground. Here the company did have a clear product alternative—the other electric vehicles on the market, the most successful of which to date has been the Tesla. But it had no market alternative. Public transportation, Zipcars, cell phones— they were all analogies. There was no budget to repurpose any- where. Moreover, on the product side, where Renault took the lead with the first car, the end result was not sufficiently compel- ling to attract enough consumers to utilize the infrastructure at anything like an economic capacity. The whole effort ended up twisting slowly in the wind and was wound down in 2013.

In Closing

In light of these cautionary tales, let me just close this section with a word of warning. If you try out this exercise of choosing the competition, and have trouble finding either a single, clear market alternative, or a credible second vendor leveraging your type of disruptive technology, this is a clue. It means that you are probably not ready to cross the chasm.

Chasm crossing requires a single target beachhead segment, and in that segment, there needs to exist already the budget dollars to buy your offer. To be sure, the budget will be "mis- named," because it will be allocated to some brain-dead, ineffec- tive Band-Aid approach to solving what has become a broken, mission-critical process. But it must exist, or else you will lose a full year just in educating the market to put aside money that might be used to buy your product in the following year.

Choosing your market alternative wisely is the solution to this problem. But it has to be credible. And understand that, as soon as you call out your choice, you are in for a fight. That market alternative, whoever it may be, had plans for the money you are targeting. Indeed, it considers that budget as *its* budget, and it will not take kindly to your actions.

That's where the product alternative comes in. You need to make clear to everyone involved that a technology shift is under way here and that old solutions simply cannot hope to keep up. Trade magazines on their best day cannot be interactive. Direct mail programs on their best day cannot catch me at the golf course. General agents on their best day cannot provide round-the-clock answers to consumer questions—at least not cost-effectively. It is not your intent to deride the performance of the established Old Guard. Indeed, you should honor it, as your target customer has long-standing relationships with these vendors. Rather, it is to suggest that a new wave is coming, and that you intend to domesticate that technology to the same ends as these tried-and-true solution providers.

So, market alternatives call out the budget and thus the market category, and product alternatives call out the differentiation. It sounds a lot like positioning, the topic to which we will now turn.

Positioning

Creating the competition, more than anything else, represents a watershed moment in positioning. Positioning is the most discussed and least understood component of high-tech marketing. You can keep yourself from making most positioning gaffes if you will simply remember the following principles:

1. *Positioning, first and foremost, is a noun, not a verb.* That is, it is best understood as an attribute associated with a company or a product, and not as the marketing contortions that people go through to set up that association.
2. *Positioning is the single largest influence on the buying decision.* It serves as a kind of buyers' shorthand, shaping not only their final choice but even the way they evaluate alternatives leading up to that choice. In other words, evaluations are often simply rationalizations of preestablished positioning.
3. *Positioning exists in people's heads, not in your words.* If you want to talk intelligently about positioning, you must frame a position in words that are likely to actually exist in other people's heads, and not in words that come straight out of hot advertising copy.
4. *People are highly conservative about entertaining changes in positioning.* This is just another way of saying that people do not like you messing with the stuff that is inside their heads. In general, the most effective positioning strategies are the ones that demand the least amount of change.

Given all of the above, it is then possible to talk about *positioning* as a verb—a set of activities designed to bring about *positioning* as a noun. Here there is one fundamental key to success: When most people think of positioning in this way, they are thinking about how to make their products *easier to sell*. But the correct goal is to make them *easier to buy*.

Companies focus on making products easier to sell because that is what they are worried about—selling. They load their marketing communications with every possible selling argument, following the age-old axiom that if you throw a lot of mud at a wall, some of it is bound to stick. Prospective customers shrink from this barrage, which in turn causes the salespeople to chase after them that much harder. Even though the words appear to address the customers' values and needs, the communication is really focused on the seller's attempt to manipulate them, a fact that is transparently obvious to the potential consumer. It's a complete turnoff—all because the company was trying to make its product easy to sell instead of easy to buy.

Think about it. Most people resist selling but enjoy buying. By focusing on making a product easy to buy, you are focusing on what the customers really want. In turn, they will sense this and reward you with their purchases. Thus easy to buy becomes easy to sell. The goal of positioning, therefore, is to create a space inside the target customer's head called "best buy for this type of situation" and to attain sole, undisputed occupancy of that space. Only then, when the green light is on, and there is no remaining competing alternative, is a product easy to buy.

Now, the nature of that best-buy space is a function of who is the target customer. Indeed, this space builds and expands cumulatively as the product passes through the Technology Adoption Life Cycle. There are four fundamental stages in this process, corresponding to the four primary psychographic types, as follows:

1. *Name it and frame it.* Potential customers cannot buy what they cannot name, nor can they seek out the product unless they know what category to look under. This is the minimum amount of positioning needed to make the product easy to buy for a technology enthusiast.

The goal here is to create a technically accurate description of the disruptive innovation that puts it into its ontologically correct category with a descriptive modifier that sets it apart from the other members of that category. Think Linnaeus cataloging the world of biological organisms.

Here are three such examples of naming and framing:

- Verinata is a genetic test that isolates and analyzes fetal cells extracted from a mother's blood sample to detect Down syndrome.
- HANA is a database system that operates in memory in its entirety, eliminating performance bottlenecks associated with writing to disk, reading from disk, or rehosting data into a data warehouse.
- Nicira is a software-defined network in which the network configuration and control plane is moved out of the routing and switching equipment to run on a server instead, where it can manage the entire network from a single point of control.

If you are not technically informed about these categories, these positioning statements are not likely to mean a lot to you. But for the experts in the field, they are definitive. That's what you need to communicate with technology enthusiasts.

2. *Who for and what for.* Customers will not buy something until they know who is going to use it and for what purpose. This is the minimum extension to positioning needed to make the product easy to buy for the visionary.

Visionaries do not care about the ontology of the new innovation—they care about its potential impact. What disruptive change can it enable in their environment that they can leverage for dramatic competitive advantage?

If we apply this standard to the three examples above, we would generate positioning statements like the following:

- For expectant mothers, their doctors, and their health-care insurers, Verinata provides a pregnancy screening test that is less painful, safer, and cheaper than amniocentesis, while delivering the most accurate results in the industry.
- For business process owners and the IT organizations that support them, HANA enables real-time analytics to be applied to transactions as they are unfolding, redirecting them to optimized outcomes that could not otherwise be achieved.
- For network administrators operating in a cloud computing environment, Nicira enables rapid reconfiguration of a single network fabric to meet the dramatically different performance needs of multiple mission-critical applications.

The key idea here is to focus on the *So what?* and the *Who cares?* part of the value proposition. If the *who* has the clout and the budget, and the *what* is a big enough reward, then the risk of sponsoring an early market purchase is worth taking.

3. *Competition and differentiation.* Customers cannot know what

to expect or what to pay for a product until they can place it in some sort of comparative context. This is the minimum extension to positioning needed to make a product easy to buy for a pragmatist.

This is by definition a post-chasm situation, for the category is now sufficiently viable that there are multiple vendors competing to fill the same budget.

In the prior pages we talked about how when crossing the chasm you have to "create" the competition, leveraging the intersection of a market alternative and a product alternative. That is a special case. The more general case, and the one more familiar to marketing agencies with whom an entrepreneur might be working, is for more established markets. There the goal is to position offerings relative to their adoption status. Consider the following examples:

- In the category of smartphones, Apple iPhones are the design leader, Google Android phones are the price/performance leaders, while RIM BlackBerry phones are a fading star and Microsoft Windows 8 phones a late entry.
- In the category of enterprise collaboration software, Jive is strongest in IT-led deployments, Yammer in end-user grassroots deployments, and Salesforce's Chatter in customer-oriented communication applications.
- Among public cloud computing services, Amazon Web Services is far and away the market leader, with Rackspace providing an open-source alternative, and Microsoft specializing in hosting cloud versions of its own enterprise software offerings.

These sorts of distinctions help a generalist sign off on technology purchase decisions by creating points of reference with "adopters like me."

4. *Financials and futures.* Customers cannot be completely secure in buying a product until they know it comes from a vendor with staying power who will continue to invest in this product category. This is the final extension of positioning needed to make a product easy to buy for a conservative.

   Microsoft, IBM, Oracle, Intel, SAP, EMC, and Cisco are all long-standing blue-chip companies with whom conservatives feel comfortable. Dell and HP have both put themselves behind the eight ball here with sustained underperformance in recent years. Sun got so far behind it had to get acquired by Oracle.

These four positioning strategies correspond to the four quadrants of the Positioning Compass. The key takeaway from this section is that positioning is more about the audience's state of mind than yours. Most failed positioning statements arise from vendors being unable to see themselves from someone else's point of view.

The Positioning Process

When positioning is thought of primarily as a verb, it refers to a communications process with four key components:

1. *The claim.* The key here is to reduce the fundamental position statement—a claim of undisputable market leadership within a given target market segment—to a two-sentence format outlined later on in this chapter.

2. *The evidence.* The claim to undisputed leadership is mean-
   ingless if it can, in fact, be disputed. The key here is to
   present sufficient evidence as to make any such disputation
   unreasonable.

3. *Communications.* Armed with claim and evidence, the goal
   here is to identify and address the right audiences in the
   right sequence with the right versions of the message.

4. *Feedback and adjustment.* Just as football coaches have to
   make halftime adjustments to their game plans, so do
   marketers, once the positioning has been exposed to
   the competition. Competitors can be expected to poke
   holes in the initial effort, and these need to be patched
   up or otherwise responded to.

This last component makes positioning a dynamic process
rather than a one-time event. As such, it means marketers revisit
the same audiences many times over during the life of a product.
Establishing relationships of trust, therefore, rather than wowing
them on a one-time basis, is key to any ongoing success.

The Claim: Passing the Elevator Test

Of the four components, by far the hardest to get right is the
claim. It is not that we lack for ideas, usually, but rather that we
cannot express them in any reasonable span of time. Hence the
elevator test: Can you explain your product in the time it takes
to ride up in an elevator? Venture capitalists use this all the time
as a test of investment potential. If you cannot pass the test, they
don't invest. Here's why:

1. *Whatever your claim is, it cannot be transmitted by word of mouth.* In this medium the unit of thought is at most a sentence or two. Beyond that, people cannot hold it in their heads. Since we have already established that word of mouth is fundamental to success in high-tech marketing, you must lose.

2. *Your marketing communications will be all over the map.* Every time someone writes a brochure, a presentation, or an ad, they will pick up the claim from some different corner and come up with yet another version of the positioning. Regardless of how good this version is, it will not reinforce the previous versions, and the marketplace will not get comfortable that it knows your position. A product with an uncertain position is very difficult to buy.

3. *Your R&D will be all over the map.* Again, since there are so many different dimensions to your positioning, engineering and product marketing can pick any number of different routes forward that may or may not add up to a real market advantage. You will have no clear winning proposition but many strong losing ones.

4. *You won't be able to recruit partners and allies,* because they won't be sure enough about your goals to make any meaningful commitments. What they will say instead, both to each other and to the rest of the industry, is "Great technology—too bad they can't market."

5. *You are not likely to get financing from anybody with experience.* As just noted, most savvy investors know that if you can't pass the elevator test, among other things, you do not have a clear—that is, investable—marketing strategy.

So how can we guarantee passing the elevator test? The key is to define your position based on the target segment you intend to dominate and the value proposition you intend to dominate it with. This is the *who for and what for* positioning statement that resonates with visionaries and kicks off the early market competition. At the same time, you also want to foreshadow your mainstream market future, leveraging the *competition and differentiation* positioning we discussed relative to market and product reference competitors.

Here is a proven formula for getting all this down into two short sentences. Try it out on your own company and one of its key products. Just fill in the blanks:

- For (target customers—beachhead segment only)
- Who are dissatisfied with (the current *market alternative*)
- Our product is a (product category)
- That provides (compelling reason to buy).
- Unlike (the *product alternative*),
- We have assembled (key whole product features for your specific application).

Let's try this out with a few examples, starting with some we have already looked at earlier in the chapter.

Verinata
- For older pregnant mothers and others
- Who want an alternative to amniocentesis to screen for Down syndrome
- Verinata provides a genetic analysis of fetal DNA
- That does not involve inserting a needle into the womb.

- Unlike other genetic tests for fetal abnormalities,
- The Verinata test is the most accurate on the market.

HANA

- For online retailers and others
- Who want to better assist their customer agents to upsell and cross-sell consumers during their purchasing transactions,
- HANA is a database for online transaction processing
- That supports applying analytics in real time to determine the very best offer to make.
- Unlike database solutions from Oracle, the market leader,
- HANA does not require melding and maintaining two separate environments for transaction processing and analytics.

Now what is often interesting about writing a statement like this is not what you write down but what you have to give up. In the case of Verinata, there is nothing about it being the cheapest test. And in the case of HANA, there is a narrow focus on retailers even though we know there are many other applications for in-memory databases outside of retail. Wouldn't it have been better in both cases to have included extra value statements for a bigger effect?

The answer here is an emphatic *no*. Indeed, this is just what defeats most positioning efforts. *Remember, the goal of positioning is to create and occupy a space inside the target customers' head.* Now, as we already noted, people are very conservative about what they let you do inside their head. One of the things they do not like is for you to take up too much space. This means they will use a kind of shorthand reference: Mercedes ("top-of-the-line, conservative"), BMW ("upscale performance sedan, yuppie"), Lincoln ("American top-of-the-line, tired"), Lexus ("New kid on the block, current best buy"). That's all the space you get for your primary differentiation statement. It's like a telegram with less than one line. If you don't make the choice to fill the space with a single attribute, then the market will do it for you. And since the market includes your competition trying to de-position you, don't count on it to be kind.

One final point on claims before moving on to other issues: *The statement of position is not the tagline for the ad.* Ad agencies come up with taglines, not marketing groups. The function of the statement of position is to control the ad campaign, to ensure that however "creative" it may become, it stays on strategy. If the point of the ad is not identical with the point of the claim, then it is the ad, not the claim, that must be changed—regardless of how great the ad is.

The Shifting Burden of Proof

The toughest thing about high-tech marketing is that just about the time you get the hang of something, it becomes obsolete. This is even true of something as innocent as providing evidence. That is, like everything else in high tech, the kind of evidence that is needed evolves over the course of the Technology Adoption Life Cycle. This can be summarized within the structure of the Competitive Positioning Compass:

POSITIONING: THE EVIDENCE

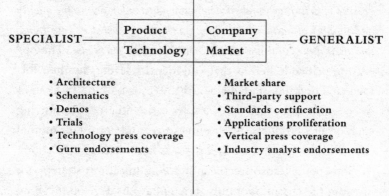

By working your way up the left and then up the right of the compass, you can trace the evolution of desired evidence as the market evolves from the technology enthusiast to the visionary to the pragmatist and conservative. The key point to notice is the transition from product to market, corresponding to crossing the chasm. This is simply a corroboration of a point we have been making all along, that pragmatists are more interested in the market's response to a product than in the product itself.

What is particularly awkward for a high-tech company making this transition is that for the first time the major sources of desired evidence are not directly under its control. This is not a matter of having the right features or winning the right benchmark war.

It is a matter of other people—theoretically disinterested third parties—voting to endorse your product not only in word but in deed. It is actual investment in building the whole product that demonstrates to the pragmatist that, if you are not already the market segment leader, you are destined to become so.

In sum, to the pragmatist buyer, the most powerful evidence of leadership and likelihood of competitive victory is market share. In the absence of definitive numbers here, pragmatists will look to the quality and number of partners and allies you have assembled in your camp, and their degree of demonstrable commitment to your cause. The operating principle here is that you identify leaders by their followers. The kind of evidence this buyer is looking for is signs of co-marketing, such as joint sales calls and cross-referencing each other's products in sales literature, and consistent mutual support even when the other party is not present in the room.

This point leads directly into communications strategy for crossing the chasm. Not only do you have to develop this kind of evidence of whole product support; you also have to make sure that everyone hears about it.

Whole Product Launches

The concept of a *whole product launch* is a derivative of the widely known practice of a product launch. That is, whenever a new high-tech product is introduced, it is customary to launch it by first briefing the industry analysts and long-lead press editors well in advance of the launch date (so they can serve as references), and then taking the top company executives on a tour to the weekly trade press the week prior to announcement, with the announcement itself capped by an event.

These product launches work just fine when the product itself is "new news." Then they are an appropriate tool for the development of early markets. By the same token, however, they are not appropriate for crossing the chasm. At this point the product is not new news—at least it had better not be if we are planning to win over the pragmatist buyer. The trade press is not interested, therefore, in a great trumpeting article on Release 2.0, not even if you are Oracle, SAP, or Microsoft. So if the message is not "Look at my hot new product," then what is it going to be, and how are you going to get it out?

The message that will resonate now is much more likely to be "Look at this hot new market." This message typically consists of a description of the emerging new market, anchored by a new approach to a problem stubbornly resistant to conventional solutions, fed by an emerging set of partners and allies, each supplying a part of the whole product puzzle, to the satisfaction of an increasingly visible and growing set of customers. The lure embedded in this story is that we are seeing a new trend in the making, and everyone who has a seat on this bandwagon is going to be in on the Big Win. This is a great story for small entrepreneurial companies to be able to tell because it gives them a credibility that they cannot achieve on their own. Their product does not even have to be the centerpiece of the whole product—it just has to be an indispensable component, as was ATI's GPU (graphics processing unit) to the Microsoft Xbox 360, or the ARM technology that lives at the heart of Apple's iPhones.

Now, how can marketing communications improve your odds of winning such a position? First, marketers have to pick the right communications venue. There are two venues, in general, that lend themselves to whole product stories. The first is the business press. Whole product stories, particularly ones sparked by partnerships and alliances coming together to bring off some wonderful result for a particular company, are the bread and butter of business fare. Companies organizing to bring off this feat consistently, and thereby dominate a particular market segment, are particularly of interest.

If the company is brand-new, to be sure, the business press is leery. In this instance it is important first to build some references in the financial analyst community, based not on the company per se but on the market opportunity it has in its sights. Financial analysts are usually quite open to briefings on emerging market opportunities, and in that context, can be wooed to take an interest in an emerging entrepreneurial venture. Once they have bought into the market, then they can be used as a reference point by the business press in developing a story.

In bringing this story to the business press, it is important to bring along as many of the other players in the market as possible. One effective tactic is to hold a press conference with multiple spokespersons on the dais—customers, analysts, partners, distributors, and so on. A more elaborate version of the same approach is to sponsor a conference on the core issue that is driving the development of this market. The key objective in either case is to communicate the bandwagon effect in progress.

Finally, communicating via the business press has to be done within the framework of a big idea. Technology stories, told at the level of technology, are only interesting as vignettes, squibs to be used as filler between the main articles. For a technology story to be a *business story*, it has to be about something that transcends high tech. Typically, the seed of the story is either a new type of opportunity or problem that can now be addressed effectively because of advances in the industry. These advances will have been sparked by technology breakthroughs, and that will be part of the story, but they are now seen to extend to the entire whole product infrastructure, and that will be the main thrust of the story.

The great benefit of the business press as a medium of communication is its high degree of credibility across virtually all business buying situations. This is a two-edged sword for the entrepreneurial company. In order to preserve its credibility, the business press is reluctant to endorse entrepreneurial enterprises until they have been well proved. It takes a long time, in other words, to earn coverage. On the other hand, having broken through in this medium once, it is much easier to do so again. Furthermore, subsequent product-oriented coverage in the trade press tends to become more thorough as the company attains greater stature in the business press.

So building relationships with business press editors, initially around a whole product story, is a key tactic in crossing the chasm. In addition to the business press, the other communications channel for getting out a whole product message is what could be loosely termed "vertical media"—that is, media specifically dedicated to a particular industry or a particular profession. Industry trade shows and conferences, meetings of professional associations, and publications dedicated to a specific market segment all tend to attract pragmatists and conservatives, people who put a high value on maintaining relationships within their group. These associations are relatively open to participation from supporting vendors, provided that the vendors are not too obtrusive with their sales messages.

Whole product issues are ideal for this kind of communication. The idea is to get in a room with a number of people in a given industry and outline the current state of technology innovation in the vendor's marketplace as it relates to their business. Correctly framed, these sessions put the customer, rather than the vendor or the vendor's product, at the center of things. They align themselves with the customer's needs and the alternatives available to meet those needs. Thus, although they are at one level clearly self-serving to the vendor, they do not *feel* self-serving, positioning the vendor more as a consultant than as a salesperson.

The goal of a whole product launch campaign, overall, is to develop relationships in support of a positive word-of-mouth campaign for your company and products. The first thing to remember is that developing these relationships takes time—time to ferret out who are the key influencers, time to get to know them on more or less equal footing, time to get up to speed on the industry issues so that the relationship is pertinent and valuable to both parties. The other thing to remember is that, once these relationships are in place, they represent a major barrier to entry for any competitor. Pragmatists and conservatives—the core of any mainstream market—like to do business with people they know.

Recap: The Competitive Positioning Checklist

To define the battle effectively so that you win the business of a pragmatist buyer, you must:

1. Focus the competition within the market segment established by your must-have value proposition—that is, that combination of target customer, product offering, and compelling reason to buy that establishes your primary reason for being.

2. Create the competition around what, for a pragmatist buyer, represents a reasonable and reasonably comprehensive set of alternative ways of achieving this value

proposition. Do not tamper with this set by artificially excluding a reasonable competitor—nothing is more likely to alienate your pragmatist buyer.

3. Focus your communications by reducing your fundamental competitive claim to a two-sentence formula and then managing every piece of company communication to ensure that it always stays within the bounds set out by that formula. In particular, always be sure to reinforce the second sentence of this claim, the one that identifies your primary competition and how you are differentiated from it.

4. Demonstrate the validity of your competitive claim through the quality of your whole product solution and the quality of your partners and allies, so that the pragmatist buyer will conclude you are, or must shortly become, the indisputable leader of this competitive set.

7

Launch the Invasion

In this chapter the final pieces of the D–Day strategy come into play—distribution and pricing. As we launch our invasion across the chasm, distribution is the vehicle that will carry us on our mission, and pricing is its fuel. These two issues are the only two points where marketing decisions come into direct contact with the new mainstream customer. Decisions in both distribution and pricing, therefore, have enormous strategic impact, and, with distribution in particular, there is typically only one chance to get it right. For this reason, we have put these two last in our invasion planning sequence, so that we could have the advantage of nailing everything else down first.

The number-one corporate objective, when crossing the chasm, is to secure a distribution channel into the mainstream market, one with which the pragmatist customer will be comfortable. This objective comes before revenues, before profits, before press, even before customer satisfaction. All these other factors can be fixed later—but only if the channel is established. Or, to put it the other way around, if the channel is not established, nothing further can be accomplished. Finally, given that establishing the channel is the number-one goal, the fundamental function of pricing during this same period is to achieve this same end. In other words, during the chasm period, the number-one concern of pricing is not to satisfy the customer or to satisfy the investors, but to *motivate the channel*.

To sum up, when crossing the chasm, we are looking to attract *customer-oriented distribution* with one of our primary lures being *distribution-oriented pricing*.

Customer-Oriented Distribution

The world of high-tech sales, marketing, and distribution has been changing dramatically over the past decade, largely due to the increasing impact of the World Wide Web. What has not been changing, on the other hand, are the customers these distribution channels are targeting. Essentially, these group into five classes, each of which is associated with an optimal approach:

1. *Enterprise executives* making big-ticket purchasing decisions focused on complex systems to be adopted broadly across their companies,
2. *End users* making relatively low-cost purchasing decisions focused on personal or workgroup technologies to be adopted locally and individually,
3. *Department heads* making medium-cost purchasing decisions for use-case-specific solutions that will be adopted within their own organization,
4. *Engineers* making design decisions for products and services to be sold to their company's customers, and

5. *Small business owner-operators* making modest purchase
   decisions that are nonetheless highly material to them,
   given limited capital to spend and a strong need to get
   value back.

Each one of these groups has a preferred channel of distribution. Let's see how each plays out.

Direct Sales and the Enterprise Buyer

Enterprise buyers making major systems purchases expect to pay hundreds of thousands or millions of dollars. In that context they are looking for a consultative sales experience that identifies their key needs and custom-fits the vendor's offering to meet them. The direct sales approach meets this expectation via a top-down approach to marketing, sales, and delivery.

The marketing involved is called *relationship marketing*. It typically consists of thought leadership events designed to attract a handful of senior executives to a forum in which they can learn from experts, exchange ideas with each other, and connect with the vendor's senior staff. This is followed up with personal contacts, often leading to a referral down into the organization to explore a possibility raised in an earlier conversation.

Once the sales motion is under way, the normal approach is called *solution selling*, in essence a whole-product tailoring job to meet the specific needs of a particular prospect. In the early market, however, prospects may not even be aware they have a need to address. This can call for something we call *provocation-based selling*, in which the vendor makes the provocative claim that the customer should redirect existing budget, typically to meet a heretofore unnoticed opportunity or impending crisis. In either case the vendor will be sending a highly accomplished executive to meet first with a senior member of the prospect company's management team to ascertain if there is sponsorship and then with various middle managers to do a needs analysis and develop a proposal. From there the goal is to win the nod and get the contract through purchasing, the PO signed, and the work under way.

During the delivery phase of this go-to-market approach, all the tailoring that was promised in the proposal has to be delivered in fact. This typically requires the vendor to field its own professional services team, focused primarily on installing the vendor's products, often supplemented by a third-party systems integrator who takes responsibility for all the peripheral reengineering and integration needed to get the entire solution up and running.

Companies that have leveraged the direct sales approach to cross the chasm and achieve meteoric growth beyond it include Salesforce.com, VMware, and WorkDay.

Web-Based Self-Service and the End-User Buyer

In total contrast to enterprise buyers, end users purchasing technology for themselves expect to pay perhaps hundreds of dollars per purchase or tens of dollars per month—and that is often after a free trial. In that context they are looking for a transactional sales experience that is primarily self-service. The World Wide Web is terrific at providing just that.

Marketing on the Web is primarily *promotional marketing*, often driven by a free offer or trial period. It is typically driven by click-through advertisements and targeted email, which are becoming increasingly effective as marketers leverage techniques like behavioral targeting, machine learning, and other algorithmic technologies to improve their connection rates.

Once a user clicks on a link, the state of the relationship changes to a *direct response* sales activity. This may be culminated at first contact or more frequently through a series of contacts that allow end users to test the waters before they commit. With digital service offerings, there is often a free trial period or a minimally configured offer that is provided completely free of charge. This is the so-called *freemium* model, where revenue is generated by upselling customers to added-value offerings after they have adopted the core technology for free. On the other hand, if the offer consists of a physical product rather than just software bits, then the sale is typically an e-commerce transaction as modeled by Amazon, the world leader in this mode of selling, including a shopping cart, checkout process, shipping and handling options, and email confirmation and tracking notices.

Support in this world of transactional selling is designed around avoiding personal contact, something that saves the vendor money and often pleases the customer as well. The lowest common denominator here is a website with FAQs (frequently asked questions), backed up by an email address for other support queries, and for more responsive vendors, a chat service where a single support professional can serve multiple customers simultaneously. At the top of the heap here is community-enabled tech support of the type provided by Lithium, Jive, and others, where knowledgeable customers lend a helping hand to new arrivals.

It is questionable whether companies that have had success with this model have to cross a chasm or not. We present an alternative model for describing their market development path in an appendix at the end of this book, titled "The Four Gears Model for Digital Consumer Adoption." Companies who have managed these four gears to a successful outcome include the Internet communications company Skype, the enterprise collaboration company Yammer, and next-generation presentation company Prezi.

Sales 2.0 and the Department Manager Buyer

Departmental buyers making IT purchases are caught in a bind. Because they are part of a larger enterprise, they need systems that pass muster in that context. But they have neither the budget nor the staff to support such acquisitions. Historically they have had to settle for cobbled-together solutions of highly variable quality delivered by local value-added resellers. But the Internet and the Web have created a powerful new sales channel alternative, what some are calling Sales 2.0.

Sales 2.0 consists of direct-touch marketing, sales, and service conducted entirely over digital media. The marketing looks a lot like the Web-based self-service transactional marketing for end users. The difference arises when the prospect clicks on a link. Instead of going to an automated response system, the click alerts a human salesperson who then approaches the end user via email, chat, or a voice call. Based on the prospect's level of interest, this can lead to a referral to a website, a download of relevant literature, an invitation to a webinar, or a Web-enabled live demo of the offer. As prospects demonstrate increasing levels of engagement, the system tracks their status and alerts salespeople to the next step in the sales cycle. The entire process, from interest to close, is conducted over the Web.

Once the prospect becomes a customer, responsibility shifts from the sales to the delivery team. In the new world of software-as-a-service, vendors are much more incented to follow through on their promises because their customers are a click away from discontinuing their subscriptions. These dynamics are well described in *Consumption Economics*, by Todd Hewlin, a longtime colleague, and J. B. Wood, a longtime friend. These economics have driven vendors to increasingly efficient and effective ways of delivering digital support, both directly and through community-enabled pathways as well. And for those situations where physical presence is required, Sales 2.0 companies recruit partners to address on-site support needs.

Companies that have succeeded with this model include the accounting software vendor Intacct, the legal software application vendor IntApp, the cloud computing vendor Rackspace, and the collaboration software vendor Box.

Traditional Two-Tier Distribution and the Design Engineer

Design engineers make for very demanding prospects and customers. They do not like marketing communications or salespeople, but they need the services of both if they are to stay on top of the latest component technologies they may want to design into their next product. Moreover, from the vendor's point of view, despite their demanding requirements, they don't actually have any authority to purchase product in volume; instead they are a critical early decision maker as to whether the vendor gets invited to the purchasing table at all. So, lots of work, no money on the table—what's the good part?

Well, from a marketing point of view, the good news is that the Web is a terrific medium for communicating with these folks. They can engage or disengage as they like and can get a factual perspective on almost any issue they care to research. Sooner or later, however, they need to see samples, and more often than not this is sufficiently complex to require a human sales presence on-site. That is what brings the customer-touching "second"

tier of a two-tier distribution channel into play, typically independent manufacturers' representatives. This channel, however, does not have the capital to hold inventory, so it in turn is
supported by a first-tier, vendor-facing organization, typically
called a distributor.

Once the designer has selected a given component, that trig-
gers what the component vendors call a *design win*. This is an
invitation to negotiate with the product company's purchasing
department to set price, terms, and conditions for a set of future
purchases, the volume of which will depend on the success or
failure of the new product in its market. Support during this
phase of the relationship transfers directly to the component
vendor, who often fields sophisticated engineers to collaborate
in debugging the customer's next-generation designs.

This sales and marketing model is arguably the oldest in all
of the high-tech sector. Anchored by distributors like Avnet,
Arrow Electronics, and Tech Data, it is the channel of choice
for companies like Intel, Broadcom, and NVIDIA, all three of
whom make silicon components for smart devices.

Value-Added Resellers and the Small Business Owner

Small business owners are really just consumers wearing a different hat. Their challenge is that their business needs do not
fit neatly into consumer buckets, and so they find themselves
slogging through outlets like Fry's and Office Depot trying to
figure out what to buy and how to work it. They know they
need help, but they don't have deep pockets, so they are always
looking for a way to get things done on the cheap.

Their natural allies in this quest are local value-added resellers, often sole proprietors themselves, who run low-overhead
businesses that are always hungry for new customers. Often

such VARs are themselves technology enthusiasts, happiest when they can share their expertise with others and get paid for it to boot. What they are not typically good at, on the other hand, is marketing and sales. This is where the product vendors have to step in.

Vendors who target the truly small business customer must take virtually all of the responsibility for marketing, and most of it for sales, while almost none for post-sales support—this last is what the VAR really does for a living. The marketing consists of classic Web programs, with the added wrinkle that the lead flow may be shared directly with the VARs if the latter have an active go-to-market capability. The small business customer cannot really leverage a Sales 2.0 experience because they lack the expertise to participate in it knowledgeably. Instead, they are looking for an agent to mediate between them and the world of technology, a trusted advisor, and that is the role the VAR fulfills. And because VARs make the bulk of their income from post-sales services, they are anxious to earn and keep that trust.

Companies that have had success with this model include small-business-CRM SaaS-provider Infusionsoft, online bill payer Bill.com, and Intuit, the latter two companies leveraging CPAs as their primary VAR resource.

To sum up, there are five distinct customer-oriented distribution channels serving high tech, each aligned with a different kind of target customer, each of which will have a different slant to your compelling reason to buy. Entrepreneurs crossing the chasm need to pick the channel that best fits their target market strategy. That will be their primary channel. As the company succeeds on the other side of the chasm, it will likely expand its channel coverage to take on other segments, but for a long time to come its primary channel will not change. It is important, therefore, that the channel/strategy fit be a good one, and there is no shame in switching channels if your first choice is not bearing proper fruit.

Distribution-Oriented Pricing

Pricing decisions are among the hardest for management groups to reach consensus on. The problem is that there are so many perspectives competing for the controlling influence. In this section we are going to sort out some of those perspectives and set out some rational guidelines for pricing during the chasm period.

Customer-Oriented Pricing

The first perspective to set on pricing is the customers', and, as we noted in the section on discovering the chasm, that varies dramatically with their psychographics. Visionaries—the customers dominating the early market's development—are relatively price-insensitive. Seeking a strategic leap forward, with an order-of-magnitude return on investment, they are convinced that any immediate costs are insignificant when compared with the end result. Indeed, they want to make sure there is, if anything, *extra money* in the price, because they know they are going to need special service, and they want their vendors to have the funding to provide it. There is even a kind of prestige in buying the high-priced alternative. All this is pure *value-based pricing*. Because of the high value placed on the end result, the product price has a high umbrella under which it can unfold.

At the other end of the market are the conservatives. They want low pricing. They have waited a long time before buying the product—long enough for complete institutionalization of the whole product, and long enough for prices to have dropped to only a small margin above cost. This is their reward for buying late. They don't get competitive advantage, but they do keep their out-of-pocket costs way down. This is *cost-based pricing*, something that will eventually emerge in any mainstream market, once all the other margin-justifying elements have been exhausted.

Between these two types lie the pragmatists—our target customers for the chasm-crossing effort. Pragmatists, as we have said repeatedly, want to back the market leader. They have learned that by so doing they can keep their whole product costs—the costs not only of purchase but of ownership as well—to their lowest, and still get some competitive leverage from the investment. They expect to pay a premium price for the market leader relative to the competition, perhaps as high as 30 percent. This is *competition-based pricing*. Even though the market leaders are getting a premium, their allowed price is still a function of comparison with the other players in the market. And if they are not the market leader, they will have to apply the reverse of this rule and discount accordingly.

From the customer perspective, then, as we argued in the previous chapter, the key issue when crossing the chasm is market leadership versus a viable competitive set, captured by comparison to your two reference competitors, and the key pricing strategy is premium margin above a norm set by these comparisons. That is, you have earned a premium over the market alternative because you have next-generation technology and a premium over the product alternative because you have invested to orchestrate a segment-specific whole product.

Vendor-Oriented Pricing

Vendor-oriented pricing is a function of internal issues, beginning with cost of goods, and extending to cost of sales, cost of overhead, cost of capital, promised rate of risk-adjusted return, and any number of other factors. These factors are critical to being able to manage an enterprise profitably on an ongoing basis. None of these, however, has any immediate meaning in the marketplace. They take on meaning only as they impact other market-visible issues.

For example, vendor-oriented pricing typically sets the distribution channel decision by establishing a price-point ballpark that puts the product in the direct sales, Web self-service, or Sales 2.0 camp. Moreover, once the product is in the market, vendor-oriented factors can make a big impact if, for example, they allow for a low-cost pricing advantage in a late mainstream market, or if they allow for operating margins that can fund new R&D for the next early market.

The biggest impact of vendor-oriented pricing is on the number of transactions required to create a given amount of annual revenue. Suppose the target were $10 million, which if it came from a single beachhead segment is a reasonable revenue stream to suggest you have successfully crossed the chasm. In an OEM model fulfilled through two-tier distribution, that could be the result of just one or two big design wins. In a direct sales model, it is probably more like twenty to forty transactions, with half of it coming from perhaps the top five. In a Sales 2.0 model, you would probably multiply that by ten—say, 200 to 400 transactions. And in a VAR-enabled model going after small businesses, multiply by another ten, and for a consumer high-volume model, still another ten—say, 20,000–40,000 transactions averaging around $25/month.

As you can see, each of these price points will call into being a different management perspective on the sales funnel, top to bottom, from suspect to prospect to qualified lead all the way to closed customer. The higher the volume, the more transactional the process, and the more you depend on filling the top of the funnel. The higher the price, the more relationship-oriented the process, the more you focus on the bottom of the funnel. And, yes, with Sales 2.0 you do tend to focus most on the middle of the funnel, where process effectiveness and efficiency have their biggest impacts.

That all said, vendor-oriented pricing represents the least sound basis for pricing decisions during the chasm period. This is a time when you must be almost entirely externally focused—both on the new demands of the mainstream customer and the new relationship you are trying to build with a mainstream channel. Indeed, because of the primary importance of securing ongoing means of access to the mainstream, this latter issue should be the number-one factor for pricing decisions during this period.

Distribution-Oriented Pricing

From a distribution perspective, there are two pricing issues that have significant impact on channel motivation:

- Is it priced to sell?
- Is it worthwhile to sell?

Being priced to sell means that price does not become a major issue during the sales cycle. Companies crossing the chasm, coming from success in the early market with visionary customers, typically have their products priced too high. Price does become an issue with the pragmatist customer, but when the channel feeds back prospect resistance and uses comparable products as evidence of the expected pricing, companies too often argue that they have no such competition, and that the channel does not know how to sell the product properly.

However, products can also be priced too low to cross the chasm. The problem here is that the price does not incorporate sufficient margin to reward the channel for the extra effort required to introduce a disruptive innovation into their already established relationship with a mainstream customer. If the channel is going to go out of its way to take on something new, the reward has to be significantly more attractive than whatever is available from business as usual.

If we put all these perspectives together and look at them in a crossing-the-chasm context, the fundamental pricing goal should be as follows: Set pricing at the market leader price point, thereby reinforcing your claims to market leadership (or at least not undercutting them), and build a disproportionately high reward for the channel into the price margin, a reward that will be phased out as the product becomes truly established in the mainstream, and competition for the right to distribute it increases.

Recap: Invasion Launching

To sum up, the last step in the D-Day strategy for crossing the chasm is launching the invasion—that is, putting a price on your product and putting it into a sales channel. Neither of these actions resolves itself readily into a checklist of activities, but there are four key principles to guide us:

1. The prime goal is to secure access to a customer-oriented distribution channel. This is the channel you predict that

mainstream pragmatist customers would expect and want to buy your product from.

2. The type of channel you select for long-term servicing of the market is a function of the price point of the product. If this is not direct sales, however, then during the transition period of crossing the chasm, you may need to adopt a supplementary or even an alternative channel—one oriented toward demand creation—to stimulate early acceptance in the mainstream.

3. Price in the mainstream market carries a message, one that can make your product easier—or harder—to sell. Since the only acceptable message is one of market leadership, your price needs to convey that, which makes it a function of the pricing of comparable products in your identified competitive set.

4. Finally, you must remember that margins are the channel's reward. Since crossing the chasm puts extra pressure on the channel, and since you are often trying to leverage the equity the channel has in its existing relationships with pragmatist customers, you should pay a premium margin to the channel during the chasm period.

This list of principles not only concludes this chapter but also brings to a close chapters 3 through 7, on marketing strategy for crossing the chasm. The goal of these chapters has been to lay out a framework of marketing ideas to assist companies in meeting the challenges of the chasm period. The D-Day strategy, as a whole, seeks to emphasize both the great peril and the great opportunity that lie before a company in this situation. The greatest impediment to action in such situations is often a lack of understanding of the appropriate alternatives. Hopefully, these chapters have gone some distance toward removing that impediment.

There is, finally, a larger set of issues that come into play. For if the chasm is a great challenge—and it is—it is one that is in large part self-imposed. To put it simply, our industry makes the chasm worse than it has to be. Until we understand how we do so, and stop doing so, we will never really master the chasm.

With this thought in mind, let us turn to our conclusion, "Leaving the Chasm Behind."

Conclusion:

Leaving the Chasm Behind

It has long been fashionable to talk about how high-tech companies can and should become market-driven organizations. My own view, however, is that there is not any *becoming* involved. All organizations *are* market-driven, whether they acknowledge it or not. The chasm phenomenon—the rapid acceleration in market development followed by a dramatic lull, occurring whenever a discontinuous innovation is introduced—drives all emerging high-tech enterprises to a point of crisis where they must leave the relative safety of their established early market and go out in search of a new home in the mainstream. These forces are inexorable—they *will* drive the company. The key question is whether management can become aware of the changes in time to leverage the opportunities such awareness confers.

Thus far we have been treating the chasm as a market development problem and have focused exclusively on marketing strategies and tactics for crossing it. But the impact of the chasm extends beyond the marketing organization to every other aspect of the high-tech enterprise. In this final chapter, therefore, we are going to step back from the marketing view and look at three other critical arenas of change: finance, organizational development, and R&D. Our goal throughout is to guide behaviors that keep the enterprise moving forward into the mainstream marketplace and not, as so often happens, letting it fall back into the chasm.

The fundamental lesson of this chapter is a simple one: *The post-chasm enterprise is bound by the commitments made by the pre-chasm enterprise.* These pre-chasm commitments, made in haste during the flurry of just trying to get a foothold in an early market, are all too frequently simply unmaintainable in the new situation. That is, they promise a level of performance or reward that, if delivered, would simply destroy the enterprise. This means that one of the first tasks of the post-chasm era may well be to manage one's way out of the contradictions imposed by pre-chasm agreements. This, in turn, can involve a major devaluation of the assets of the enterprise, significant demotions for people who are unsuited to the responsibilities implied by their titles, and marked changes in authority over the future of the product and technology—all of which is likely to end in bitter disappointments and deep-seated resentment. In short, it can be a very nasty period indeed.

The first and best solution to this class of problems is to avoid them altogether—that is, *avoid making the wrong kind of commitments during the pre-chasm period.* By looking ahead at the outset, while we are still in the early market phase, to where we must go in order to survive the chasm crisis, we can vaccinate ourselves against making the kind of crippling decisions that doom so many otherwise promising high-tech enterprises.

Let me acknowledge that this is much harder to achieve than it looks. I am reminded of the many times as an adolescent when

I was sagely advised that I was making some very bad choices because I was "going through a phase." I loathed that advice. First, it made me feel vaguely inadequate and rather inferior to the person giving it. And second, even though I suspected it to be true, it was totally useless information. I might be going through a phase, but since I was in the phase, and was therefore doomed to perform in some incompetent way, what good was this knowledge? How could I stop being myself?

That, however, is exactly what the high-tech enterprise must accomplish to leave the chasm behind. It must stop "being itself"—in the sense that it must accept that it is going through a phase and act competently with that knowledge.

To leave the chasm behind, there is a molting process that must occur, a change of company self, wherein we grow away from celebrating familial feelings and dashing individual performances and step toward rewarding predictable, orchestrated group dynamics. It is not a time to cease innovation or to sacrifice creativity. But there is a call to redirect that energy toward the concerns of a pragmatist's value system instead of a visionary's. It is not a time to forgo friendships and implement an authoritarian management regime. Indeed, management style is one of the few things that can remain constant during this period of transition. But there is a call to review and revalue the skills and instincts and talents that helped to build a winning position in the early market in light of the impending challenge of building one in the mainstream. And that call can and will test friendships and egos throughout the firm.

The principles and practices for successful post-chasm management of financial, organizational, and product development issues are all significantly different from their pre-chasm counterparts, and not everyone is adaptable or amenable to the changes required to operate in the new order. The good news is, in either case, there will always be plenty of jobs. That is, while individual high-tech enterprises have shown a very erratic track record over the past three decades, the sum total of revenue and employment of the industry as a whole has grown dramatically. We all need to remember this during the chasm reshuffling.

Specifically, our goal is to establish a new set of behavioral norms, not to convert individuals to a new style of behavior. Our job is to provide a framework for helping individuals understand for themselves where they will best fit in and then let them take appropriate action. Some transitions may have to be forced—there really is no time to dillydally—but even then, one can hope to redirect talent to a more natural home for itself.

With that thought in mind, let us turn to the first and most influential set of decisions that post-chasm enterprises inherit from their pre-chasm selves—the financial ones.

Financial Decisions: Breaking the Hockey Stick

The purpose of the post-chasm enterprise is to *make money*. This is a much more radical statement than it appears.

To begin with, we need to recognize that this is *not* the purpose of the pre-chasm organization. In building an early market, the fundamental return on investment is *investor risk reduction*, accomplished through converting an amalgam of technology, services, and ideas into a replicable deployable offering and proving that there are customer use cases that create a demand for this offer. Early market revenues are one measure of this demand, but they are typically not—nor are they expected to be—a source of profit. As a result, the early market organization is not required to adopt the discipline of profitability.

Nor does the pre-chasm organization motivate itself by profitability, or typically any other financial goal. Oh, to be sure, there are the get-rich dreams that float in and out of idle conversation. But there are much headier rewards closer at hand—the freedom to be your own boss and chart your own course, the chance to explore the leading edge of some new technology, the career-opening opportunity to take on far more responsibility than any established organization would ever grant. These are what really drive early market organizations to work such long hours for such modest rewards—the dream of getting rich on equity is only an excuse, something to hold out to your family and friends as a rationale for all this otherwise crazy behavior.

So early market entrepreneurs are not called to focus on, nor are they oriented toward, making money. This has enormous significance, as most management theory assumes a profit motive present, serving as a corrective check against otherwise alluring tactics. When that motive is not present, people make financial commitments that have consequences they either do not, or do not care to, foresee. Although this comes in many and varied forms, perhaps its most prevalent one is the *hockey stick forecast of revenue growth*.

Entrepreneurs may be many things when it comes to financial issues, but they are typically not slow on the uptake. If venture capitalists are the ones with the money, and a hockey stick forecast is one of the rules you follow to get that money, then they will be sure to follow those rules. And so entrepreneurs raise capital using "hockey stick" graphs of revenue attainment.

That is, they bring forward a business plan that shows no revenue development for some period of time—as long as they possibly can defer—after which there is a sharp inflection in the curve, and rapid, continuous, and what any sane person would call miraculous revenue growth from there on. As a form, it is as precise and conventional as a love sonnet—and just as likely to get one into trouble.

Hockey stick curves are created by spreadsheets, a software tool that many have argued has driven some of the worst investment decisions in our sector's history. It is so easy to increment a revenue number by a percentage and just let the software take it from there. Now in theory, this revenue line approximates a real profile of how the company could capitalize on a developing market opportunity. As such, it would serve as the "master line" in the spreadsheet, the one to which all others must account. That is how profitable operations work.

In fact, however, the revenue line is a slave—and to not just one but two masters. At the front end, it is slave to the entrepreneur's cost curve, and at the back, to the venture capitalist's hockey stick expectations. Revenue numbers, under this methodology, are . . . well, whatever they have to be. Once that sum is identified, then market analyst reports are scoured for some appropriate citations, and any other source of evidence or credibility is enlisted, to justify what is a fundamentally arbitrary and unjustifiable projection of revenue growth.

Now, if the current model of high-tech market development were not flawed, this might work, or at least work better or more often. But in fact, the revenue development that actually occurs looks more like a *staircase* than a hockey stick. That is, there is an initial period of rapid revenue growth, representing the development of the early market, followed by a period of slow to no growth (the chasm period), followed by a second phase of rapid growth, representing return on one's initial mainstream market development. This staircase can continue indefinitely, with the flat periods representing slower growth due to transitioning into adjacent mainstream segments, and the rapid rises representing the ability to capitalize on those efforts. As more and more segments are served, sooner or later the ups and downs begin to cancel each other out, and one can achieve the less bumpy results that Wall Street greatly prefers. (In fact, only the most successful high-tech companies have achieved such a state; most continue to fluctuate more dramatically than the financial community can understand, with the result that their stocks routinely take a vicious beating at the slightest indication of bad news.)

All this is well and good. The staircase model is perfectly viable—unless you have mortgaged your stake in the company on making the hockey stick scenario come true. That, unfortunately, is precisely what most high-tech funding plans commit to. And when the hockey stick scenario does not come true, and the mortgage comes due, the founder's equity gets radically diluted, things fall apart, and the company dies in the chasm. That is the course sketched out in the high-tech parable in chapter 1 of this book.

Now, the venture community has long been aware of this problem. Cynics in high tech believe they count on it—that's how the "vulture capitalists" take over the company from the unwitting entrepreneur. But the truth is, such a strategy is a lose-lose proposition, and most investors know it. They may call it "the valley of death" instead of the chasm, but they know it is there. All they have to do is look at their own portfolios.

The question now becomes, if we have the chasm model to work with, what can we do differently? This question really breaks into two parts—one directed to the financial communities that provide the sources of capital, and the other to the high-tech executives who provide the sources of management. For the former, the key issue is how to reformulate its concepts of valuation and expected rate of return, and for the latter, it is when to spend capital and when to adopt the discipline of profitability. Let's look at both of these more closely.

The Role of the Venture-Financing Community

All investment is a bet on performance against competition within time. What the chasm model surfaces is a need to rethink these variables. From the investment point of view, the most pressing question initially is, How wide is the chasm? Or, to put this in investment terms, How long will it take before I can achieve a reasonably predictable ROI from an acceptably large mainstream market?

The simple answer to this question is, as long as it takes to create and install a sustainable whole product. The chasm model asserts that no mainstream market can occur until the whole product is in place. A reasonable corollary, I believe, is that once the whole product is in place—in other words, has become institutionalized—the market will develop quickly—normally, although not necessarily, around the company that drove and led the whole product effort.

Can we predict how long this will take? I think so. By analyzing the target customer and the compelling reason to buy, and then dissecting all the components of the whole product, we can reduce this process to a manageable set of performance factors, each of which can be projected ahead in time, with an estimated point of convergence. It's not a science, but it's not a black art, either: It is, in essence, just another kind of business plan.

Supposing this plan has some credibility, a raft of other questions immediately follow. How big will this market be? Again, the simple answer is, As big as can be motivated by the target market's use case—its compelling reason to buy—as served by the whole product. Market boundaries occur, in other words, at the point of failure of either the value proposition or the whole product. By contrast, the other market-making factors—alliances, competition, positioning, distribution, and pricing—do not impact the size of market but rather the rate of market penetration. Given free market economy incentives, efficient solutions in these areas will fall into place sooner or later if the market is truly there.

If all the preceding assertions are true—and that is certainly something that warrants further investigation in any specific case—then all the key factors of the investment decision are reasonably out in the open, and the decision itself can be made without having to consult the entrails of a sacrificial animal. Estimates of market size, rate of penetration, cost to achieve market leadership, and anticipated market share can all be made in the light of day, without smoke and without mirrors. There will still be plenty of room for disagreement about probability of success and degree of risk, but there should not be any fundamental leap of faith demanded.

So the call to action to the investment community is, Make your client companies incorporate crossing the chasm into their business plans. Demand to see not only broad, long-term market characterizations but also specific target customers for the D-Day attack. Drive them to refine their value propositions until they are truly compelling, and then use these to test how many target customers there truly are. Force them to define the whole product, and then help them to build relationships with the right partners and allies. Again, use the results to test hypotheses about market size. As for competitive sets and positioning, beware of pushing your small fishes too soon into big ponds. And as for distribution and pricing, don't look for "standard margins" until the chasm has truly been crossed. To sum up, use the crossing-the-chasm matrix of ideas to ensure proper management of financial assets.

The Role of the Venture-Managing Community

Now let's turn to the entrepreneur's key concern: How long should I live off of venture capital, and when should I adopt the discipline of break-even cash flow? The bounds of this decision work as follows. Until break-even cash flow is achieved, nothing is secure, and your destiny is not under your own control. This argues for early adoption of the profitability path. In fact, in slow-developing markets with low capitalization requirements, there is a very strong case for adopting profitability from day one. Early visionary customers will pay consulting fees and prepay royalties to help fund low-capitalization start-ups. From an accounting view, these prepaid royalties cannot be booked immediately as revenue, but they can make you cash-flow positive from day one, and thus keep 100 percent of the equity reserved for a later date.

The great benefit of adopting the discipline of profitability at the outset is that you do not have to learn it later on. All too frequently, even when they are led by experienced managers, enterprises that are venture funded for long periods of time fall into a "welfare state mentality," losing their sense of urgency, and looking for their next paycheck to come from yet another round of financing instead of from the marketplace.

Moreover, the discipline of profitability teaches you to "just say no" early and often. For most ideas there simply isn't any money to fund them. The enterprise is forced to focus drastically just because of resource constraints. This radically reduces time to market because people are not focused on doing something else and because they understand it is the market that is paying their paychecks. And finally, when one does go seeking external capital, there is no stronger evidence for a high company valuation than it having already demonstrated not only real market demand but also its own ability to process that demand profitably.

Indeed, the case for seeking profitability from the beginning is so strong, you begin to wonder why you would ever not choose this route. Essentially, there are two reasons. First, the price of category development and market entry is often simply too great to fund with sweat equity or consulting contracts. This is clearly the case in any manufacturing-intensive operation. Today, however, with the move to outsourced manufacturing, when companies like Cisco ship as much as 45 percent of their products *without ever touching them*, when fabless semiconductor companies use foundries for all their goods, and when there is even such a thing as a chipless semiconductor company, Rambus, which simply licenses a patented memory interface architecture, it is more a matter of getting the team on board and the engineering in place than it is putting in place a line or ramping up inventory. Still, there are always real costs associated with a physical goods business model, and they will inevitably exceed a pay-as-you-go budget, so a lot of venture funding goes to supporting just this sort of enterprise.

The other reason to forgo initial profitability is when the category is expected to develop so rapidly that you cannot afford to grow organically as a bit player. The explosion of the Internet has created a land-grab mentality heretofore unknown, and everyone is racing to beat out competitors in capturing market share. Google's capturing the number-one position in search, Amazon's achievement in retail and more recently in Web services, and Facebook's success in social networking all have translated into dramatic surges in market capitalization that have left their competitors seemingly permanently behind. In that kind of game, the race really is to the swiftest, and second prize is a long way back from first, so spending early and big is seen as the key to success.

Beyond this there is a third, more general principle that can help entrepreneurs think through their management of capital for marketing purposes. In this realm, it is typically more capital intensive to cross the chasm than it is to build the early market. Early market development efforts typically do not respond well to massive infusions of capital—in the 1980s we saw this with the IBM PC Jr. and Prodigy; in the 1990s with pen-based computers and video-to-the-home, in the last decade with RFID chips for inventory management and smart grids for electric power distribution. You simply cannot spend your way into the hearts and minds of technology enthusiasts and visionaries.

To be sure, there is a minimum level of capitalization required. You have to be able to travel to make direct sales calls, and show up looking presentable, and you probably should have an office and a phone that is answered in a professional way. You do need to invest in early market public relations—the product launch is crucial to building early market success—but you do not need to advertise, nor do you need to invest in developing partnerships or building channel relationships. All this is premature until you have established some early market credibility on your own.

Once early market leadership has been established, however, the entire equation changes. The whole product investment—securing the partnerships and alliances and then making them work to deliver the final goods—takes a significant number of funded initiatives. So does the channel development process, both on the pull and on the push sides, creating demand and providing incentives for sales. And it is critical during this period to have an effective marketing communications program, including press relations, market relations, and advertising.

In sum, this is when you want to spend your market development money—not before. It is important, therefore, that you not start this process until after you have established early market leadership, and that you not commit to throwing off all kinds of cash during the chasm period. Simply applying these two concepts to the business plan can keep you out of a lot of trouble.

Organizational Decisions: From Pioneers to Settlers

Turning from issues of finance to issues of people, we must recognize that the chasm inherently separates visionaries from pragmatists—not only among the customers for technology-based offerings but also among the companies that serve them. To leave the chasm behind, to cross it and not fall back into it, involves a transformation in the enterprise that few individuals can span. *It is the move from being pioneers to becoming settlers.*

In the development organization, pioneers are the ones who push the edge of the technology application envelope. They do not institutionalize. They do not like to create infrastructure. They don't even like to document. They want to do great deeds, and when there are no more great deeds to be done, they want to move on. Their brilliance fuels the early market, and without them, there would be no such thing as high tech.

Nonetheless, once you have crossed the chasm, these people can become a potential liability. Their fundamental interest is to innovate, not administrate. Things like industry standards and common interfaces and adaptations to installed solutions, especially when these solutions are clearly technically inferior, are all foreign and repugnant to the high-tech pioneers. So as the market infrastructure begins to close in around them, they are already looking for less crowded country. In the meantime, they are not likely to cooperate in the compromises needed and can be highly disruptive to groups that are seeking to carry this agenda out. It is critical, therefore, that as the enterprise shifts from the product-centric world of the early market to the market-centric world of the mainstream, pioneer technologists be transferred elsewhere—either to another, more futuristic project within the enterprise, or if that is not an option, to another company where their talents can be better utilized.

There is a comparable process going on in the sales force at the same time. Here the group at the forefront is the high-tech sales pioneers. These are people who have the gift of selling to visionaries. They are able to understand the technology and product at a level where they can readily manipulate it and adapt it to the dreams of the visionaries. They can talk the visionaries' language, understand the quantum leap forward that visionaries seek to achieve, and wrap their products in that cloak. They can translate that language back into concrete manifestations of the product, to be illustrated through custom demos, for which they make insatiable demands. They can think big, and they can get big orders. They are the darlings of the early market. Without them, achieving early market leadership is all but impossible.

These same people, however, also become a liability once you have crossed the chasm. Indeed, they are the ones primarily responsible for dragging companies back into the chasm. The problem is, they cannot stop making the visionary sale, a sale predicated on delivering custom implementations of the whole product. Such contracts are fulfilled by robbing from Peter—the mainstream R&D effort—to pay Paul—the custom R&D effort necessary to achieve the visionaries' buying objective. The key to leaving the chasm behind is to stop custom developments and institutionalize the whole product, to build to a set of standards that the marketplace as a whole, or at least one segment of it, can support. This mainstream effort necessarily puts enormous strain on the R&D department, who must not, therefore, be distracted by yet another wild and crazy venture. And so it is that a pioneer salesperson left unchecked can be highly disruptive and demoralizing to a sales organization looking to leave the chasm behind.

So now we have two sets of people—technology pioneers and pioneer salespeople—who are fundamental to success in the early market and potentially a liability after the company has crossed the chasm. They must be outplaced, but who is competent to do so? And how in the world will their knowledge ever be replaced? And who is going to take over what they leave behind? And is any of this moral or fair, given their contributions to date?

I know of no high-tech firm that has not struggled with

these issues sooner or later. And how you respond affects not only those who leave but also those who stay. This is a time when you must perform impeccably.

Let's deal with the moral issue first. And let us take as our starting point that casting aside people, dislocating their lives and threatening their livelihood, is immoral—even if businesses and governments routinely do so with abandon. The issues then become ones of foresight, agreement, planning, and preparation. Pioneers do not want to settle down. That is not in their best interest nor in the interest of the companies that employ them. If, at the beginning of the process, everyone can acknowledge this fact, and acknowledge that the very goal of pioneers, the final manifestation of their success, is to create a mainstream market and thereby put themselves out of a job, then we can have a reasonable basis for going forward. How we would go forward and under what kind of compensation program is a discussion we need to postpone until we look at how to make the transition to the other side of the equation, to the settlers who are expected to come in and take their place.

The truth is, of course, that settlers do not take pioneers' places. They take other places, ones that pioneers have never occupied nor would ever choose to. Nonetheless, settlers do take over the employment roster, including the management positions, the authority, and ultimately the budget. And they build fences and create laws (called procedures) and do all the things that led to range wars between pioneers and settlers back in the Old West. All this bodes well for the post-chasm marketplace, populated with pragmatists, who like reliable, predictable people and abhor surprises. But it hardly sits well with the pioneers. How in the world, then, can you make the transition between these two groups in an orderly way?

Two New Job Descriptions

The key is to initiate the transition by introducing two new roles during the crossing-the-chasm effort. The first of these might be called the *target market segment manager,* and the second the *whole product manager.* Both are temporary, transitional positions, with each being a stepping-stone to a more traditional role. Specifically, the former leads to being an industry marketing manager, and the latter to a product marketing manager. These are their "real titles," the ones under which they are hired, the ones that are most appropriate for their business cards. But during the chasm transition they should be assigned unique, one-time-only responsibilities, and while they are in that mode, we will use their "interim" titles:

The target market segment manager has one goal in his or her short job life—*Transform a visionary customer relationship into a potential beachhead for entry into the mainstream vertical market that that particular customer participates in.* If Citicorp is the client, then it is banking; if Aetna, insurance; if DuPont, chemicals; if Intel, semiconductors. The process works like this:

Once you have closed such an account as part of an early market sales program, assign the target market segment manager as its account manager with a charter that allows him the kind of extensive customer contact that will let him really learn how their business works.

- He must attend the trade shows, read the literature, study the systems, and meet the people—first, just within the one account, and subsequently, in related companies.
- At the same time, he must take over the supervision of

the visionary's project, make sure it gets broken up into
achievable phases, supervise the introduction and rollout of the early phases, get feedback and buy-in from
the end users of the system, and work with the in-house
staff to spin off the kind of localized implementations
that give these initial deliverables immediate value and
impact.

- At the same time, he will be working with the whole
product manager to identify which parts of the visionary project are suitable for an ongoing role in the whole
product and which are not. The goal is to isolate the
idiosyncratic elements as account-specific modifications,
making sure thereby not to saddle the ongoing product
development team with the burden of maintaining them.

The market segment manager should not be expected to
generate additional revenue from the account in the short term,
because the visionaries believe they have already paid for every
possible modification they might need. What he can be expected to do, however, is the following:

- *Expedite the implementation of the first installation of the
system.* This not only contributes to the bottom line,
as it will expedite the purchase of additional systems;
it also secures the beginning of a reference base in the
target market segment. Most companies fail miserably
in this regard, so much so that even several years later
their initial "big name" accounts cannot be referenced.
The key here is to remember that pragmatists are not
interested in hearing about who you have sold to but
rather who has a fully implemented system.

- *During the implementation of the first installation, introduce into the account his own replacement, a true account manager, a "settler," who will serve this client, hopefully, for many years to come.* Note that at this point the pioneer salesperson is still in the picture, still has the relationship with the visionary, but the day-to-day operation of the account is entirely in others' hands. This is typically just fine with the pioneer, for he recognizes this to be the kind of detail-oriented settler work for which he has no liking.

- *Leverage the ongoing project to create one or more whole product extensions that solve some industry-wide problem in an elegant way.* The intent is either to absorb these elements into the product line or to distribute them informally as an unsupported product extension through a users' group. Either way, such add-ons increase the value of the product within the target market segment and create a barrier to entry for any other vendor.

The Whole Product Manager

While the target market segment manager is pursuing these tasks in the customer's environment, there is a corresponding internal role to be filled. Here the transition is from product manager to product marketing manager via the short-lived role of whole product manager. These titles are all sufficiently alike as to be confusing, so let's take a minute to sort out three very different jobs.

A *product manager* is normally a member of the development organization who is responsible for ensuring that a product gets created, tested, and shipped on budget, on schedule, and according to specification. It is a highly internally focused job, bridging the marketing and development organizations, and requiring a high degree of technical competence and project management experience. Occasionally companies try to relocate this job into the marketing organization, in an effort to be more market driven, but this ploy inevitably encounters organizational resistance—if not organ transplant rejection—and thus rarely succeeds.

A *product marketing manager* is always a member of the marketing organization, never of the development group, and is responsible for bringing the product to the marketplace and making it accessible to the distribution channel. This includes all the elements on the crossing-the-chasm agenda, from target customer identification through to pricing. It is a highly externally focused job.

Not all organizations separate product managers from product marketing managers, but they should. Combining the jobs almost always results in one or the other simply not getting done. And the type of people who are good at one are rarely good at the other.

Now, the *whole product manager* is a product-marketing-manager-to-be. The reason she is not one today is that the job itself is premature. Until there is a successful crossing of the chasm, there are no meaningful market relationships or understandings to drive the future of product development. The target market segment manager is off getting these under way, but they are not there today. What is there today, on the other hand, is a list of bug reports and product-enhancement requests that is growing with disconcerting speed. *If this list is not managed properly, it will bring the entire development organization to its knees.*

The tactic, which at once secures proper management of

the list and initiates a transition process from pioneer to settler culture in the development side of the house, is to take this list away from the product manager and give it to the whole product manager. For whoever is serving as the product manager at this point almost certainly is a pioneer—otherwise, the organization could not have got to where it is today.

The problem with this person continuing to direct the future of the product is that she will be driven first and foremost by her own personal commitments made to early customers. Unfortunately, these commitments are often not in the best interest of the mainstream market customer. To be sure, they must eventually be fulfilled—unless they are to be negotiated away—but in either case, they should not be given automatic priority over other issues. What should increasingly become the prioritizing factor for on-going product development work is contribution to mainstream, pragmatist customer satisfaction—in other words, contribution to the whole product—hence, the need to transfer authority.

Once this authority is transferred, the enterprise has taken a key step in moving from a product-driven to a market-driven organization. As the shape of the mainstream market emerges, as the needs of this market can be increasingly identified through market research and customer interviews, then the whole product manager steps into the title that she has had all along on her business card, product marketing manager. To try to take this step earlier in the market development cycle is foolish. During the early market it is important to be product-driven and to give strong powers to the product manager. But to fail to take those powers back now is equally foolish, for every day that the enhancement list is in the hands of the original pioneers, the company risks making additional development commitments to unstrategic ends.

To sum up, at the beginning of the chasm period, the organization is dominated by pioneers, with strong powers invested in a few top-gun salespeople and product managers. By the time we are into the mainstream market, that power should be distributed far more broadly among major account managers, industry marketing managers, and product marketing managers. This gradual dissemination of authority will ultimately frustrate the pioneer contributors, hampering their ability to make quick decisions and rapid responses. Ultimately, it will make them want to leave.

Coping with Compensation

This brings us back, full circle, to the fundamental issue that underlies so much of the frustration and disappointment that builds up within high-tech organizations—compensation. Few compensation programs recognize either the fundamentally different contributions of pioneers and settlers or their fundamentally different tenures within the enterprise, and thus these programs end up discriminating against one or the other. And when compensation programs do discriminate—when they discourage the very behaviors that ought to be rewarded, or vice versa—then organizations fail.

To work through all the complexities of designing appropriate compensation schemes is beyond both the scope of this book and the capabilities of its author. I can only sketch out a few general principles that seem important to follow.

Let's start on the sales side. A typical pioneer sale involves a broad purchase agreement, predicated on successful implementation of a pilot project. Even when there has been a major up-front payment, the rational way to book this business is to defer recognizing the larger order until it has been confirmed. That could be at least a year away, and during that period, we will have introduced a number of new players into the account, including the target market segment manager. The pioneer salesperson might even be gone by then. Say some account manager just joins the firm, inherits the account, and all of a sudden the flood of orders come in. What is the appropriate way to compensate?

The key is to discriminate between *account penetration* and *account development*. The latter is a more predictable, less remarkable, longer-abiding achievement. Compensation here should reward such things as longevity of the relationship, customer satisfaction, and predictability of revenue stream. It should be spread out over time and not clumped into dramatic payments. Because there is high value associated with the intangibles of the ongoing customer relationship, much of it can be based on an objectives-based formula rather than pure revenue attainment. If equity is part of the compensation strategy for the firm as a whole, it is a reasonable component here as well, provided it is doled out slowly, with the larger portions coming at the end of the program, to reward stability of service. Overall, however, since this is not a high-risk role, it should not be a high-reward one, either.

By contrast, compensation for account penetration by a pioneer salesperson should have the opposite characteristics. It should provide the bulk of its rewards immediately, in recognition of a single key achievement—winning the account. This is an extraordinary event, one that few can accomplish, and it is critical to determining the firm's long-term future. It is an extraordinarily high-risk endeavor, with the odds stacked heavily against the salesperson. It therefore deserves extraordinary compensation. On the other hand, if it was achieved by promising more than anyone can deliver, perhaps even more than anyone really knew, then that is not behavior we want to reward. So, although we would like the compensation to be front-loaded, there must also be a reality check built into the process. Because the pioneer salesperson will be moving on, we do not want an extended compensation program, and thus equity, for example, is an inappropriate vehicle. Taking all this together, the situation argues for a bonus-based program more than a straight commission approach—something lucrative for the salesperson, event-driven and over and done with relatively quickly, and not so closely tied to revenue recognition that either the pioneer has to overstay his or her welcome in order to reap the rewards or earns an extraordinary cash reward at a time when the company simply cannot afford that sort of outlay.

Compensating Developers

Moving over to the development side, there is one remaining compensation challenge—the pioneer technologists. These divide into two camps—true company founders and very early employees. The former have bet their lives on the equity gamble, and there is nothing further to discuss, except to hope that in reading this book they learn to conserve a large portion of that equity to fund crossing the chasm. The latter pose a real problem.

They can point with accuracy to the notion that they created a large part of the core product. Thus, should that product become a mainstream market hit, they feel they should get a major share of the gains. The fact is, they don't, and the truth is, bluntly, they don't deserve it, either. Mainstream success, as we have argued at length, is a function of the whole product, not the core product, and that is a very large team effort indeed.

What pioneer technologists do have a right to is a larger share of the early market returns, because here it truly is the core product that drives success. The problem is that cash is typically so tight during this period, there is none to throw off in the form of a reward. So equity is the usual fallback. This is a compromise, to say the least, as equity should be reserved for people who cross the chasm and stay—not the pioneers' ideal role, but still a more frequent occurrence than them leaving the company.

To sum up, improper compensation wastes dollars and demotivates people. To be appropriate to high tech, compensation programs must take into account the differences between desired performance in the early market and in the mainstream market, as well as the types of people that can be called on to achieve these performances, and the likelihood that some of these people will need to leave the company long before it achieves significant profitability. If we can sort through these issues and come up with an appropriate distribution of rewards, we can forgo much of the agony and loss of momentum that accompany most crossings of the chasm. If we continue to operate the way we do today, we will persist in constructing self-conflicting organizations and wonder why they are not more productive.

R&D Decisions: From Products to Whole Products

At the outset of this book, we set crossing the chasm as the fundamental marketing priority in high tech. In the middle we established that institutionalizing the whole product was the fundamental strategy for succeeding in this endeavor. It is fitting, therefore, to finish up with a look at the impact of whole product marketing on long-term R&D.

R&D *is* high tech. Everything else is secondary. As an industrial sector, before anything else, we are technology-driven. Eventually we learn to create products, and then markets, and then enterprises to dominate those markets. But it starts with technology. "Build a product and they will come," to paraphrase *Field of Dreams.* That is our fundamental dream, the dynamic that drives all else.

The problem is, we grow past the dream. The products and markets and companies we create all grow up to make persistent and legitimate demands on us, and we have no choice but to serve them. And once this scenario begins, R&D doesn't get to focus on the generic product anymore. It must become *whole product R&D.*

Whole product R&D is driven not by the laboratory but by the marketplace. It begins not with creative technology but with creative market segmentation. It penetrates not into protons and processes but rather into habits and behaviors. It does not, like the captain of the starship *Enterprise,* "go where no man has gone before," but rather, like T. S. Eliot, finds the end of all its exploring is "to arrive where we started / And know the place for the first time." It prefers to assemble its creations from existing technologies and products rather than to invent new ones from scratch. Its heroes are less like Albert Einstein, who developed a whole universe out of his own head, and more like George Washington Carver, who discovered more than three hundred different uses for the peanut.

Not very heady stuff. No wonder it is so often ignored. Indeed, the word that high tech uses for whole product R&D is *maintenance.* And the people they assign to it are . . . well, the janitorial types. No top guns want to go near this stuff.

Instead, the top guns rush out to create more discontinuous innovations, flooding the market with far more technology than it can possibly absorb, and complaining all the while about how product life cycles are becoming shorter and shorter. They play the game, in other words, almost entirely to the left of the chasm, cycling through endless repetitions of early markets that never cross over to the mainstream. *Product* life cycles truly are getting shorter—but *whole product* life cycles are as long as they ever were. Ask Adobe about Photoshop or Apple about the Mac.

An Emerging Discipline

Whole product R&D is an emergent discipline. It represents a kind of convergence between high-tech marketing and consumer marketing, where, for the first time, the tools of the latter can be of significant use in solving the problems of the former. Let's look at two examples: focus groups and packaging studies.

As innovation becomes increasingly continuous, focus groups, which are virtually useless in guiding the development of an early market, become effective tools. The reason they are now effective is that the fundamental product proposition is already in the market and absorbed. Until this is the case, consumers get in way over their heads trying to anticipate the value and usage of a new high-tech product. But once that proposition is in place, the tool becomes effective. Specifically, it can be used to direct the extension and modification of an existing product line to meet the special needs of a target market segment. In this context, all consumers are asked to do is address relatively minor derivatives from a known entity—something well within their expertise. The information they give back, therefore, is valuable.

Consider another discipline that today is far more advanced in consumer marketing than in high tech—packaging. As an industry, we have considered this to be nothing more than the paint of the box, the logo, the cover. But packaging happens not just on the outside but on the inside, and the goal of good packaging is to ensure a successful experience right out of the box—an area that cries out for more research attention in high tech. Think how many dollars could be diverted into better ends that today go to expensive support services, all because our products are packaged in confusing or obtuse ways.

Now these types of efforts—focus groups and packaging studies—are traditionally located in the marketing department. But in high tech, marketing is too ignorant to drive the bus. What appears to the generalist to be a simple change may in fact cut across some fundamental technology boundary in a radically inappropriate way. Or conversely, what looks impossible to achieve may in fact be a by-product of a minor adjustment. In either case, engineering must be a direct partner in the effort, or it is wasted. It's not market research alone, nor is it just product development. It's whole product R&D, and it implies a new kind of cooperation between organizations traditionally set apart from each other.

Leaving This Book Behind

By way of parting, let us look back over the ground we have covered over the course of this book. We began by isolating a fundamental flaw in the prevailing High-Tech Marketing Model—the notion that rapid mainstream market growth could follow continuously on the heels of early market success. By analyzing the characteristics of visionaries and pragmatists, we were able to see that a far more normal development would be a chasm period of little to no growth. This period was identified as perilous indeed, giving companies every incentive to pass through it as rapidly as possible.

Taking such rapid passage as our charter, we then embarked on setting forth a strategy and set of tactics for accomplishing it. The fundamental strategic principle was to launch a D-Day type of invasion, one focused on a highly specific target segment within a mainstream marketplace. The tactics for implementing that invasion were then set out in four clusters.

To begin with, we had to *target the point of attack*, which meant isolating our target customers and their compelling reason to buy. Then we had to *assemble the invasion force*, constructed around the whole product and the partners and allies needed to make it a reality. The next step was to *define the battle*, by creating our competition and positioning ourselves, in that context, as being easy to buy. Finally, we had to *launch the invasion*, selecting our intended distribution channel and setting our pricing to give us motivational leverage over that channel.

Now we have just spent this last chapter stepping back from the immediate tactics of crossing the chasm, to look at the major commitments that get made in the pre-chasm phase of an organization's growth, thereby to guard against crippling the success of the post-chasm venture. That brings me to the end of my road. My hope is that it can be the beginning of yours.

Appendix 1

The High-Tech Market Development Model

Crossing the Chasm was first published in 1990. It was followed five years later by *Inside the Tornado*. That book completed the survey of how high-tech markets develop end to end, from the Early Market across the Chasm through the Bowling Alley into the Tornado and on to Main Street. This short appendix gives an overview of this material to help readers of this book put crossing the chasm in a broader context.

HIGH-TECH MARKET DEVELOPMENT MODEL

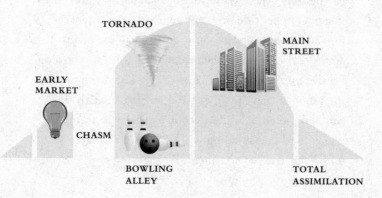

The High-Tech Marketing Model says there are five "states" of technology adoption that a market goes through from its inception to total assimilation. Here's how each one plays out:

- **The Early Market.** The customer base is made up of technology enthusiasts and visionaries who are looking to get out ahead of either an opportunity or a looming problem. The whole product is nowhere near complete, so early sales are structured as projects where the product vendor commits to do whatever it takes to make their offer work in the visionary customer's use case. Partners in this context are typically large systems vendors or systems integrators who have an established relationship with the customer company and who are putting their weight behind this effort in order to maintain that relationship. The projects are sold via direct sales, with the disruptive vendor leading the parade because it is the one that has captured the imagination—and the budget—of the visionary. Typically these deals are not price sensitive because the visionary anticipates getting an order-of-magnitude return on the investment and is willing to pay up to get there with the highest quality at the fastest speed. Competition does not yet exist, so resistance instead comes from the status quo and all the pragmatists and conservatives who believe betting this early on a disruptive innovation is just plain crazy. The disrupter and the visionary, on the other hand, are betting that they can make a tenfold difference in a critical performance metric, and that so doing will be a game changer.
- **The Chasm.** No comment. As the song says, "If you don't know me by now . . ."

- **The Bowling Alley.** This is an extension from the crossing-the-chasm beachhead into adjacent market segments where there is overlap with either the target customer's word-of-mouth community or the partner ecosystem delivering the whole product. The tactics for winning the next niche are the same as for crossing the chasm, but the time and effort required diminish as you are able to leverage past accomplishments. As new segments mature they may develop as independent niche markets or they may coalesce during the next phase of market development inside the tornado. As long as they are in the Bowling Alley phase, however, the distribution channel will be more focused on value than volume, the pricing will still maintain a premium above the commodity price point, and the competitive positioning can still be framed in terms of an intersection between the domain expertise delivered by the incumbent market alternative and the performance value delivered by a next-generation product alternative.

- **The Tornado.** This represents a dramatic "state change" in the market, something like going from water to steam. (In retrospect, to complete the analogy, you could say successfully crossing the chasm represented a conversion from ice to water.) The target customer becomes much more generic as whole sectors of the economy find themselves adopting all at the same time. The compelling reason to buy is that the new technology is now seen as must-have infrastructure, as the examples of PCs, cell phones, laser printers, websites, laptops, smartphones, and tablets all illustrate. The whole product can now be assembled at the point of sale, with partners actively adjusting their offers to ensure ease of integration into each new release of the underlying platform products. Partnerships convert to pecking orders, with some companies getting highly privileged status (Microsoft and Intel in the 1990s, Google and Apple in the past decade). Distribution is through the lowest-cost, furthest-reaching channel that can meet the service levels required to get the offer up and running. Reference pricing is no longer set by the market leader but instead shifts to the low-cost commodity provider—that is, products are priced "up" from the bottom instead of "down" from the top. Competitive positioning is no longer based on performance against targeted use cases, but instead focuses largely on price-performance of the product along with overall market share status of the company. It is still possible to play a niche game here, but the whole product has to be highly differentiated in order to withstand the erosion of commodity pricing. Winning number-one market share, especially if it is based on a proprietary technology with high switching costs, creates enormous shareholder value, as we discussed at length in *The Gorilla Game* (1999).

- **Main Street.** The tornado is characterized by double-digit—initially even triple-digit—growth rates. These last as long as it takes to deploy the first generation of infrastructure across the bulk of the landscape. Then the market shifts gears to a more sustainable rhythm, characterized by cyclical rather than secular growth, with single-digit growth rates. The commodity offer is still undifferentiated, leveraging an operational excellence strategy to target the low-cost buyer. By contrast, value-added offerings leverage a customer intimacy strategy to target market segments with discretionary income, able to pay a bit more to get a bit more. These "extra bits" fit into the existing whole product without extra effort—we call this resulting structure a "whole product + 1"—and typically priced as a 10–15 percent add-on to the base price, usually with a profit margin that is five to ten times higher than the base product. Indeed, often the base product is subsidized to secure a follow-on consumption-based revenue stream, smartphones being a conspicuous example. The ideal channel for these offers is self-serve because while the margins are great, absolute revenue is smaller, and so overhead of any kind is a profit killer. Competitive positioning is based either on incumbency (for brand leaders or products that have high switching costs) or differentiation from the commodity offer based on some secondary attribute, not typically the core functionality. This is the era when, for base case functionality, "good enough" is good enough.

As you can see, each market phase rewards a very different kind of approach. The approaches themselves are actually pretty familiar. The challenge is to get your company aligned on the right approach by reaching consensus about current market state. This can be challenging during market state transitions, as neither the state nor the best time to convert is obvious. The core lesson learned over the past two decades is this: It is better to make a coherent bet, everyone rowing in the same direction, and be wrong (because then you can change course quickly) than to delay or waffle (because you learn nothing and get a suboptimal return at every step of the way).

Needless to say, there is a lot to dig into here. So if your market and strategy need this kind of approach, you probably should spring for a copy of *Inside the Tornado*. It makes a nice companion for the book you have in hand.

Appendix 2

The Four Gears Model for Digital Consumer Adoption

Crossing the chasm is a B2B model—unapologetically. Wherever there is heavy lifting required to bring a disruptive technology to market, institutions must play an active role early in the life cycle, hence the widespread applicability of this approach. That said, as more and more technology gets deployed, it becomes increasingly possible that a new disruptive innovation could proliferate without direct engagement of any kind of institutional support. Welcome to the world of Google, Facebook, YouTube, Skype, and their ilk.

These companies also passed through an adoption process—that's how they left their legions of competitors behind—but they did not cross a chasm to do so. Instead their journey looks more like a new CPG (consumer packaged goods) offering, where trial and test markets are followed by product launches and mass-market promotions. But even here, digital is different.

Online adoption is best characterized in terms of four fundamental activities:

1. Acquire traffic
2. Engage users
3. Monetize their engagement
4. Enlist the faithful

We call this model the Four Gears, each of which makes a fundamental contribution to driving a digital enterprise to scale. That said, the process is anything but a linear progression from Gear 1 to Gear 4. Here's what happens instead:

Engagement comes first. Can you create a digital (or digitally mediated) experience that is sufficiently compelling and differentiated that end users will want to repeat it, hopefully many times over? Such repetition establishes a pattern of consumption, the first key underpinning of a mass market. You have found at least a few dogs who will eat the dog food and like it.

Once the engagement gear begins to spin, then it is time to introduce the acquisition gear. These two interact with each other, each modifying the other, as you seek to answer the second big challenge facing your fledgling enterprise: Can your compelling experience scale? This means grow both on the demand side (onboarding new users, eventually those who want something more or different from your initial users) and on the supply side (onboarding new content or product features to broaden the offering from its initial footprint). Scaling always requires modifying the offer, and modifying the offer always has an impact on scaling (though not always a happy one). This is not for the faint of heart.

That said, there is a light at the end of the tunnel, or rather, a tipping point. Tipping points are as key to consumer adoption as they are to B2B. Prior to reaching one, all efforts to scale require pumping in additional fuel—if you cut off the fuel supply, the system will revert to its initial state. But after you pass the tipping point, the system restabilizes around a new status quo, and actually pulls you forward to get you to your new "right" position. You can still screw this up (just ask the investors at Myspace or Groupon), but it takes some real effort to do so.

Given this context, the goal of the acquire-engage phase of the consumer life cycle is to get past this tipping point as quickly as possible. On the Web, depending on the size of the target market, this could call for you engaging hundreds of thousands to millions of users, on your way to even more ambitious goals. Where the tipping point actually comes is not predictable in advance—it only shows up in the rearview mirror—but when it does, when you feel the world pulling you forward rather than pushing back, then, if you have not done so already, you want to activate your enlistment gear.

Enlisting the faithful involves "hyper-engaging" with a small but vocal minority of consumers who have already demonstrated a propensity to evangelize and proselytize on your behalf. They do this because they believe in you and what you are doing so much they have made it part of their own identity. You don't pay them—indeed, to do so would be insulting; they are doing this because it has become part of who they are. It just changes the whole dynamic of the situation. This is why Simon Sinek says in his much-viewed TED talk on innovation that the goal of an innovative company is not to do business with customers who need what you have (which is indeed the goal of most established enterprises, and should be) but rather to do business with customers *who believe what you believe.*

A consumer's degree of enlistment manifests itself in three states. At its highest level, it's the kind of evangelical behavior we are talking about here. This is the key to viral marketing, where your cost of customer acquisition plummets because your existing customers act as your best marketing campaign. Think of this as the equivalent to an NPS (Net Promoter Score) of 9 or 10 ("I would definitely recommend this to a friend").

A lesser state of enlistment, one more akin to an NPS of 7 or 8 ("I would probably recommend this to a friend"), does not fuel viral marketing, but it does ensure consumer retention. This is equivalent to an entrenched brand preference—when I buy beer it is Heineken or Beck's Non-Alcoholic. I don't evangelize either brand, but they always get my business. This is the level of enlistment needed to forestall churn.

When enlistment falls below this level, one now more akin to an NPS score of 1 through 6 ("I would have reservations about recommending this to a friend"), that can signal anything from openness to switching to outright defection. Indeed, at the bottom of the range, it likely indicates counterevangelism, which is about as bad as it gets in consumer marketing, as in the 2004 film about McDonald's, *Super Size Me*.

In a consumer model, the goal of the enlistment gear is, at minimum, to keep churn below, say, 2 percent per month (giving you a lifetime customer value of about four years), and more positively, during the growth phase of the category, to catapult you into hypergrowth. You begin to work the enlistment gear, therefore, once you are confident that your engagement and acquisition gears are humming, seeking to use its acceleration to get you past your anticipated tipping point.

All this leads us to the fourth and final gear, monetization. Whereas crossing the chasm is definitely a pay-as-you-go model, the four gears represent a "URL" approach (not *uniform resource locator*, but rather "Ubiquity now, Revenue Later"). Most of the great consumer Internet successes in the first decade of this century followed this approach, introducing the monetization gear very late in the game, in some cases not until after they had sold themselves to a monetization engine (YouTube to Google, Instagram to Facebook, Tumblr to Yahoo!).

The key idea here is that monetization, regardless of when it is introduced, will slow down the other three gears. If you invoke too early or too swiftly, it is like popping the clutch on a manual transmission—you stall the engine. The art instead is to feather in the monetization gear in such a way as to minimize and absorb its retarding effects, ramping the engine back up to full speed over the least amount of time possible. In that context, the underlying goal is to determine the optimal pricing for both present and future returns, a never-ending set of experiments that must continually adapt as competition and innovation restructure the landscape.

So those are the four gears. While they evolved initially independently from, and in some sense in contradistinction to, the crossing-the-chasm model, going forward I believe the two will increasingly be invoked in a kind of pincer movement, in which grassroots movements will generate waves of mass adoption, and institutional marketing will find ways to invest and capitalize upon them. This will call on management teams to pursue two courses in parallel, with the B2C course in the lead, since until there is proven traction with the four gears, there is no material to feed the monetization engine. This pattern seems most likely to emerge in areas where public and private interests and funding intersect, such as health care, education, and public services, where both user and institutional behavior play seminal roles.

Index

About the Author

Geoffrey Moore is the author of *Escape Velocity, Inside the Tornado, Living on the Fault Line*, and other groundbreaking books for high-tech innovators and entrepreneurs.